STIMULATING SMALL FIRMS

Stimulating Small Firms

Edited by
DAVID WATKINS
New Enterprise Centre,
Manchester Business School
JOHN STANWORTH
and
AVA WESTRIP
Small Business Unit,
Polytechnic of Central London

Gower

Published by
Gower Publishing Company Limited,
Gower House, Croft Road, Aldershot, Hampshire GU11 3HR, England

British Library Cataloguing in Publication Data

Stimulating small firms.
1. Small business
I. Watkins, David II. Stanworth, John
III. Westrip, Ava
338.6'42 HD2341

ISBN 0-566-00513-1

Printed and bound in Great Britain by
Robert Hartnoll Limited,
Bodmin, Cornwall.

Contents

The cartoon on the cover of this volume is reproduced by kind permission of the Greater Manchester Economic Development Corporation Limited. It originally formed part of a poster used to draw attention to Greater Manchester Enterprize, an integrated competition and training programme sponsored by GMEDC at Manchester Business School in order to stimulate small firms within Greater Manchester County.

Introduction

This book forms part of an occasional series in which each volume collects together unpublished papers around a common theme regarding some aspect of small business in modern society. The majority of papers are the result of extensive research which often cuts across normal academic disciplines in an attempt to focus on matters of public concern and policy.

The source of many of the papers thus published (including all those in this volume) is the annual research conference of the UKSBMTA. The nine papers published here were among more than twenty presented at the September 1980 conference, which was held at Manchester Business School. Most of the papers have been extensively edited and revised for publication in the current volume. Many other excellent papers were reluctantly excluded as their subject matter did not touch directly on the current theme.

The joint editors will be happy to provide information regarding past or future conferences. Please contact: The New Enterprise Centre, Manchester Business School, Booth Street West, Manchester M15 6PB.

1 Editor's overview

Support for small firms is that <u>rara avis</u> of industrial policy - something which commands widespread support across all the major parties. The philosophy underlying such concern may vary widely, as indeed may the nature and scope of the proposed support measures. But it is clear that the small firms sector is at present 'a good thing' to all in public life and likely to remain in fashion for several years yet.

It is not difficult to see why this should be so. Both major political parties subscribed through the sixties and into the seventies to a view of industry which, broadly speaking, believed that bigger was better. Economies of scale in production, finance and markets were sought in the belief that only through the creation of organisations of a size to be internationally competitive would British industry continue to thrive in world markets. The key political questions revolved more around the ownership and control of the commanding heights of British industry, which were to bring continued growth and prosperity, than to their creation and development.

This debate continues, but it has become clear that the commanding heights look both less formidable and less attractive than they once did. Many have been scaled by foreign climbers; some famous peaks have succumbed to earthquakes. All this, plus new climbing technology, means that the demand for sherpas - and even very experienced guides - has dropped off dramatically. Small wonder then that so many vested interests see new challenges in the foothills.

It would be wrong to push the metaphor too far; would that economic change did occur on a geological timescale! But the message is clear. Just as the giantism of the sixties proved a false god, so will the faithful followers of the small firm goddess be disappointed if they believe more than a small percentage of the three million unemployed 'sherpas' can be redeployed in the short term, even with extensive retraining. One can at best hope for small miracles from small firms.

Thus it now seems timely to take stock and, on the evidence of recent research undertaken by a wide variety of individuals, throw new light on the problems and prospects of Stimulating Small Firms. For in few other important areas of economic and social policy can the research base be so thin. It is now some ten years since the Committee of Inquiry on Small Firms(1) resulted in the creation of a separate Division within the Department of Industry charged inter alia with special responsibility for monitoring the health of the small firms sector; but, despite the high hopes vested in small businesses, the statistical base upon which a considered judgement of that state of health might be made has still not been created.

While this lack of a credible data base regarding the small firm sector in Britain is a major impediment to well-tuned policy formulation, and entirely rules out certain kinds of crucial applied research, there are sometimes compensating benefits. On this theme one cannot, for example, but enjoy and admire the way SCOTT, in this current text, weaves his discussion of the failure rates of new businesses from a variety of sometimes unsuspected sources; that he is seeking answers to basic questions which should have been answered unequivocally years past seems only to enhance one's appreciation of the paper. One might go further. HALL and LAM, in examining the performance of small and newly quoted firms on the basis of readily available economic data, make one suspect that perhaps the absence of a specific small firms data base has sometimes been simply an excuse for not doing relevant research at all.

Be that as it may, no data base can ever be wholly free of the values of those who assemble it. Much (perhaps the greater part) of small firms 'research' has been, and is likely to continue to be, applied research drawing implicitly at least upon the values and special interests of those undertaking or sponsoring the work. WESTRIP demonstrates this clearly in her analysis of the changes in (and effects of) employment legislation on the small firm - a controversial area which was long seen by the Right as a main weapon in its small firm stimulation armoury.

It is clear why both Left and Right should wish to stimulate employment in small firms (and why they should differ in their approaches to policies and in their interpretation of the effects of those policies).

It is at first sight much less obvious why large firms should wish to stimulate the small business sector. Pocock(2) gave a far sighted exposition of one company's view some years ago; his company, Shell UK Limited, has continued to be in the forefront of this movement, both alone and through joint sponsorship of umbrella organisations sucn as London Enterprise Agency (LEntA). SARGENT describes the formation of LEntA and discusses the role which it and similar organisations now play from the perspective of an insider.

Local enterprise agencies and enterprise trusts are often keenly supported by the local authorities in which they are located. But, paradoxically, many of the rules and regulations which prevent the development and growth of small firms originate with those self-same authorities. WILSON's detailed study of the situation in one London borough sets the official policies and practices directed towards the small firm sector against the company-related characteristics which should determine the priorities for local authority action in Stimulating Small Firms. FALK's contribution is even more detailed. He examines the complex question of the provision of premises for small firms, recommending the provision of a range of accommodation carefully matched to the needs of firms in different phases of their development.

WATKINS and MORTON take us into the broader arena of Europe, comparing the way in which the owner-manager perceives his environment in West Germany, France and the UK. Although human nature dictates that the grass is always greener elsewhere, the clear implication of this contribution is that the scope for active stimulation of small firms is greater in this country than in two at least of our major trading 'partners'. Against this background, indication of directions in which one might wish to see the UK move are given by GIBB, whose very detailed description of the operation of small firms policy in West Germany concentrates on the most prosperous of the Länder in the Federal Republic, Baden Wurttemberg.

Broadly speaking these eight contributions are rooted in political economy. Each deals with a particular aspect of Stimulating Small Firms and, although the method and approach may vary, the implication is that by increasing the number of small firms and developing those which already exist we will achieve a situation where 'society' is in some sense better off.

But what of the individual? The characteristics of the individual small businessman have been studied in great depth and some progress has been achieved in relating personal characteristics to business success. However, a policy of Stimulating Small Firms is likely to increase not only the number of small firms but also the number of owner managers and of family units whose lives are touched - or perhaps controlled - by 'the business'.

There is some evidence(3) that the business formation process is as much an act of social expression as one of economic drive or necessity. Moreover, the same tradition of research suggests that the formation and business building processes together induce major transformations in the motivation and behaviour of the individuals concerned. One could debate the niceties of the point, but small firms policy in the UK has, by and large, been economic policy with social effects (whereas in

Germany, for example, it is as much social policy with economic effects). So it is entirely appropriate that this volume should conclude with a paper by HAYES which examines the interplay between business activity and the balance of the lives lived by the proprietors of a classic kind of small business - which has nevertheless been sadly neglected by researchers - the seaside boarding house. The author's account will doubtless reinforce both the neo-Darwinists' view that the competitive thrust of the small firms sector is the very foundation of modern economic society as much as it will delight Marxist analysts of the position of the bourgoisie in late Capitalist society. For the general reader it refocusses the mind on the main target of small firms policy - the individual owner-manager in the firm. It is all too easy to lose sight of him (or her) in the plethora of policies, agencies and incentives now seeking to stimulate the small firms sector.

David Watkins

John Stanworth

Ava Westrip

Autumn 1981

References

1. 'Committee of Inquiry on Small Firms' (The Bolton Report) Command 4811, HMSO, London, 1971.

2. 'More Jobs: A Small Cure for a Big Problem', Michael Pocock's Ashridge Lecture, Shell Small Business Unit, Shell UK Ltd, London, 1977.

3. See, for example, The Enterprising Man, O F Collins, D G Moore and D B Unwalla, Michigan State University Press, East Lancing, 1964 and Management Motivation in the Smaller Business, M J K Stanworth and J Curran, Gower Press, 1973.

2 Performance of small and newly quoted firms

GRAHAM HALL and KEITH LAM
Manchester Business School

INTRODUCTION

Support for small firms is a constituent of the industrial strategy of all the major parties and a belief that Britain's salvation lies partly in stimulating this sector has now firmly dislodged as the conventional wisdom the dogma of the importance of economies of scale in meeting international competition. As Britain sinks further into recession with the likelihood that she will always have a large pool of permanent unemployed, much of the debate on the importance of small firms centres on their ability *en masse* to generate employment rather than on the traditional measures of success such as internal rate of return or some surrogate such as return on assets.

This paper is a modest attempt to add to the debate. Part I employs Census of Production data to trace changes in the proportion that small firms contribute to the total number of firms in manufacturing industries (classified into minimum list headings (MLHs)) and changes in the proportion of employees operating in small firms. Part II considers the relationship of changes in employment and profitability to the size of quoted companies at flotation.

PART I: CHANGES IN THE IMPORTANCE OF SMALL FIRMS

PREVIOUS WORK

The current debate on the contribution of the small firm sector to the generation of employment is largely between Birch(1) on the one hand, and Fothergill and Gudgin(2) on the other. The former employed data on private US enterprises between 1969-76 to trace the relative importance to employment creation of firms of different sizes, differentiating between independent businesses and subsidiaries. He found firms with 20 employees or less to have generated 66% of net employment (gains - losses) and those with 100 or less, 82%. Most of this increase came from independent firms. Fothergill and Gudgin used data covering 1968-75 on manufacturing establishments in the East Midlands to carry out a similar exercise. Their results are not directly comparable with those of Birch, in presentation as well as coverage, but they do show that 23% of gross jobs gained (ignoring closures) came from subsidiaries of firms moving into the area, 16.5% from new firms starting up, 13% from enterprises with 25 employees or less in 1968 expanding and 31% from enterprises with 100 or less expanding. All of the net increase in employment came from new firms and those relocating. The expansion of firms employing less than 25 employees contributed less than one per cent.

Our comments on these studies are:

a) They consist of meticulous collation of large data bases but lack any theoretical content. They might well have spelt out that in the absence of synergy one might have expected the small firm sector to have experienced both a higher closure rate and a greater improvement in the level of performance[1] than the large firm sector. This follows from the assumption that a large firm is a portfolio of projects, some of which will succeed and some fail. If all these projects represented individual firms those that failed would close, whilst the performance of the survivors would, by definition, reflect that of the successful projects alone.

Synergy might, however, lead to large firms producing a better return from these portfolios than the average when the projects represented individual firms. The difficulties that small firms are traditionally supposed to encounter when attempting to raise capital might lead to some going to the wall even though their internal rate of return would have warranted an injection of cash. The finance department of a large firm might not suffer from such myopia and be prepared to supply the cash from internally generated funds. Secondly, headquarters staff might be more willing and/or able to switch resources from ailing projects as soon as the appropriate signals were received, than would small firms who might have little alternative but to stay in their present activities and hope that conditions would improve. Alternatively, projects that would simply have ended in bankruptcy if they had represented individual firms might become a drain on resources in the large firm long after a wind-up would have been warranted. Any of these models is feasible and the truth can only be established empirically.

There is no reason to suppose that such conditions had not occurred to the authors of the studies being discussed. Statistics on closure-rates were given in both cases and Fothergill and Gudgin at least (and probably Birch) were very careful to deduct employment lost through closures from survivors' net growth.

Where, however, a model might have proved useful would have been in demonstrating the significance of the differences between the performance of small firms that were independent and those that were subsidiaries of multiplant firms. The latter would represent precisely the assets of the portfolios described above.

Judging from Fothergill and Gudgin's results there are marked synergistic effects. The biggest percentage net gain in employment at 32% was enjoyed by branches of multiplant firms employing 1 to 25, four times that of independent firms of the same size. They were also more successful in two of the other three categories.

b) The classification of enterprises did not include industries. This is unfortunate because changes in the importance of small enterprises could easily be industry specific. On the one hand changes in the number of small firms operating in an industry could reflect changes in its production function. This could either arise because there was not the same scope for economies of scale or because there were net diseconomies. In some industries, for instance, large enterprises, as well as large plants, may become more vulnerable to labour disputes; in other industries, perhaps, conditions become sufficiently unstable for the flexibility of small enterprises to outweigh the usual advantages of size. The point is that neither phenomenon need be general across the economy, we might simply be observing a few special cases. On the other hand an increase in the number of small firms need not reflect changes in the production functions of their industries but of the demand function. This could occur in two ways: the increased profits resulting from a positive shift in the demand curve might attract firms of below optimum capacity. These firms would be inefficient compared to those existing already in the market but would nevertheless earn an adequate return. Alternatively, if a market were to become more fragmented much of the previous scope for economies of scale might be lost and small firms might be able to carve out their own particular niches. Again we are not talking about some general advantage that small firms possess over large and an increase in their number (or of the number of their employee) certainly need not imply that across-the-board government assistance to small firms would be a sensible policy.

c) Both studies employ as their methodology the collation of data into tables. These are obviously both necessary to present the results of any quantitative analysis and often perfectly adequate to make a particular point, but in this case it is unfortunate that they are the sole tool of analysis. Firstly, the greater the level of aggregation the more information is wasted. Secondly, tables possess all the strengths and weaknesses of graphs and uni-variable regression with the biggest weakness that interaction of the variables being considered with those omitted is ignored. For instance, if most of the relocation or expansion taking place were in particular industries, this would not be revealed by the studies being discussed even if industry-employment relationships were included on a separate table; this would not facilitate estimating the net influence of relocation or expansion after we have taken into account the industry effect. Lastly, if detailed comparisons are to be made of the entries in a table, this should be done through tests of significance, perhaps the chi-square. This is clearly more important the closer in magnitude are the numbers.

INDUSTRY ANALYSIS - RESULTS

As a first step towards establishing whether small firms are increasing in importance throughout the economy (or only in specific industries), we employed data from the Census of Production taken in 1968, 1972 and 1976. These give both the numbers of enterprises operating at various levels of employment and the numbers of employees working for enterprises of these different sizes. Thus changes can be identified in the proportion of enterprises operating within particular size-bands and/or of the number of employees employed in such enterprises.

It should be noted that 'enterprises' are the official statisticianssurrogate for 'firm'. 'Establishments' (which more or less means 'plants'), are allocated to MLHs according to their principal activity and groups of establishments operating within an MLH would be termed an enterprise. They therefore cover major divisions of companies as well as independently operating companies. Given the diversification which large firms typically exhibit this cannot be avoided if we are to consider the distribution of firms across industries.

The only employment categories common to all MLHs are above and below 100 people. This information therefore precludes discussion of very small firms; indeed, only firms employing over 25 (or in some cases 11) employees are surveyed in the Census.

The results of comparing these changes in cross-sectional data must be interpreted with caution. A rise in the number of enterprises operating in - say - the '<100' class could reflect a movement of small enterprises into an industry, either relocating or being set-up for the first time, or a reduction in the labour forces of enterprises previously in the higher category. Similarly, a reduction in the number of enterprises operating in the lower category could reflect the success of small enterprises as they expand out of the lower class. We will postpone attempting to resolve this problem until later.

Tables below show the percentage point changes in the proportion of enterprises operating with less than 100 employees and the percentage point changes in the proportion of employees operating in such enterprises 1968-72 and 1968-76. Reference to the tables shows the following:

a) Table 1 quite clearly shows over the whole or either half of the period being considered that there was virtually no fall in any industry in the proportion of small enterprises or proportion of workers employed in them. In both respects the majority of industries experienced increases, but with a markedly greater increase with regard to small enterprises. There was also a significant difference between the approximately one quarter of industries that experienced no change with respect to the proportion of enterprises and one-third with respect to employees.

b) Comparing the 'top-ten' and 'bottom-ten' between any of the tables shows very few industries in common. In other words, a dramatic rise or fall in the proportion of either enterprises or employees would have taken place in one period but not the other, and a change in the proportion of firms operating with less than 100 employees does not imply anything about the magnitude of the change in the proportion of employees employed by such enterprises. This latter point might appear counter-intuitive but is confirmed by the simple correlation coefficients of:

TABLE I

Numbers of Industries Experiencing Changes in the Proportion of Small Enterprises or Employees Employed by them

No of Enterprises 100	% Point Fall 10+	% Point Fall 5.01-10	% Point Fall 1.01-5	± 1%	% Point Rise 1.01-5	% Point Rise 5.01-10	% Point Rise 10+
1968-72	2	1	5	23	52	19	1
1972-76			4	23	50	20	6
1968-76		2	1	9	42	29	20
No of Employees Employed in Enterprises of 100							
1968-72		3	5	32	52	8	3
1972-76		2	14	35	46	6	-
1968-76		2	11	19	46	23	2

TABLE 2

LEAGUE TABLES

2A Ranking by percentage point change 1968-76 in number of enterprises operating with 100 employees

Top Ten	MLH	Percentage Point Change
Paper and Board	481	18.8
Carpets	419	15.6
Insulated wires & cables	362	15.3
Weaving of cotton etc	413	14.5
Pottery	462	13.7
Iron and steel	311/2	13.6
Electrical machinery	361	12.6
Men's and boy's tailored outwear	442	12.2
Metal-working machine tools	332	12.1
Synthetic resins etc	276	11.7
Bottom Ten		
Wheeled tractor manufacturing	380	-7.5
Telegraph & telephone equipment	363	-5.7
Spirit distilling and compounding	239	-3.4
Toilet preparations	273	-.97
Brewing and malting	231	-.91
Ordnance small arms etc	342/349	-.34
Cutlery, spoons, forks etc	392	.34
Hand tools etc	391	.42
Soap and detergent	275	.59
Animal and poultry food	219	.74

2B Ranking by percentage point change 1968-76 in number of employees working in enterprises with 100 employees

Top Ten	MLH	Percentage Point Change
Manufactured stationery	483	15.3
Metal furniture etc	399	11.3
Photographic equipment etc	351	9.7
Fur	433	9.6
Metal-working machine tools	332	9.5
Hats, caps & millinery	446	9.2
Men's & boy's tailored outwear	442	8.9
Ordnance small arms etc	342/9	8.6
Shop & office fittings	474	7.3
Miscellaneous wood & cork manufacture	479	7.2
Bottom Ten		
Wooden containers etc	475	-6.7
Household textiles etc	422	-6.1
Surgical instruments etc	353	-4.8
Lace	418	-4.6
Spirit distilling etc	239	-3.2
Leather tanning etc	431	-2.8
Hand tools etc	391	-1.8
Jute	415	-1.7
Abrasives etc	469	-1.2
Sugar	216	-1.1

1968-78	19.7
1968-72	9.2
1972-76	25.5

c) No obvious pattern emerges from the league tables. Table 2 shows those for the whole period. One can only state that three of the MLHs in the bottom ten of Table 2 are classified under 'Food, Drink and Tobacco' (Standard Industrial Classification (SIC) III) and three of those in the bottom ten of Table 2B come under 'Textiles' (SIC XIII).

INDUSTRY ANALYSIS - THE IMPLICATIONS

We have stressed the need for caution when interpreting our results. The 'top-tens' could be industries in which enterprises were contracting and the 'bottom-ten' industries in which they were expanding. To go some way to resolving this dilemma we have attempted to probe beneath the surface of the data in Table 2A by collecting information, from Extel cards and a postal survey, of a sample of the enterprises that responded to the Census of Production. This information included the number of employees in these enterprises in 1968 and 1976.

A general rise in the level of employment in the top ten would suggest that their expansion lead to the birth or relocation of new firms. A similar rise in the bottom-ten would suggest that whilst existing firms expanded new ones were not set up.

A general fall in the levels of employment in the top and bottom ten would imply that we are witnessing an unsuccessful large firm sector but in the first case its members contracted into a different size band whilst in the second this did not occur.

Additionally we calculated the percentage net change in the number of enterprises in the industries concerned, viz:-

$$= \frac{\text{No of enterprises in 1976 but not 1968 - No in 1968 but not 1976}}{\text{Total No of enterprises in 1968}}$$

If we were witnessing the renaissance of small firms we would have some expectation that this would be positive as a healthy small firm sector should least hold its own against a decline elsewhere.

Table 3 shows that enterprises in thirteen of the MLHs, seven out of the top ten, six out of the bottom ten, enjoyed an average percentage increase in the number they employed between 1968 and 1976. The high standard deviations, however, would suggest great variability in the performance in the sample. This must be partly a reflection of the low response rate in some MLHs but the standard deviation is also high where the response rate is more adequate.

When the enterprises allocated to each MLH are pooled and re-classified into size brands (Table 4), all of the latter up to the 10,000+ range exhibited an average percentage increase but the high standard deviations and lack of trend in the mean percentage changes, would suggest that no obvious relationship exists between the size of the enterprises and the employment they generated.

TABLE 3

MLH	No of responses	Mean % change	Standard deviation	% change of no of enterprises
481	17	33.8	107.3	-39.4
419	10	2.7	31.6	-16.24
362	5	-6.2	15.0	-12.8
413	13	4.5	42.5	-41.7
462	7	2.8	32.0	-12.5
311/2	14	20.2	80.5	+.6
361	22	20.6	63.5	-8.5
442	12	5.6	33.6	-22.7
332	14	-9.0	29.6	-28.6
276	9	-12.5	32.2	+4.8
380	4	15.8	12.6	-15.8
363	2	-2.4	22.6	+3.1
239	7	30.6	97.9	+20
273	8	5.7	27.1	-11.4
231	21	20.4	27.5	-42.1
392	6	42.2	56.7	-15.2
391	2	-27.3	0.2	-51.2
275	3	-15.8	16.8	+9.4
219	7	2.7	16.2	+2.4
342/349	1	-8.8	-	-31.6
	184			

This lack of evidence for the successful small firm sector apparently suggested by the Census of Production is confirmed by the generally negative net change in the number of enterprises (see Table 3) across the top and bottom ten MLHs. Had the change been positive we would have been faced with the possibility that this was the result of new large enterprises replacing those that were large or even small. As it is, enough new enterprises, of whatever size, were not entering the top and bottom ten to compensate for those leaving.

TABLE 4

No of employees 1968	Enterprises in the sample	mean % Change	S.D. %
1- 99	17	35.44	58.93
100- 199	17	6.74	33.36
200- 299	20	22.54	61.08
300- 399	16	4.77	21.79
400- 599	16	10.67	54.04
600- 999	20	0.84	31.50
1,000-1,499	20	21.92	103.24
1,500-2,499	17	1.77	41.96
2,500-4,999	14	9.27	7.99
5,000-9,999	10	11.84	30.60
10,000+	17	-4.88	15.83
TOTAL	184	11.23	55.52

PART II: THE PERFORMANCE OF NEWLY QUOTED COMPANIES

BACKGROUND

The analysis reported in Part I cast doubt on the initial impression given in the Census of Production of a dynamic small firm sector.

We do not here establish whether this doubt is justified, but we do attempt to cast fresh light on whether governments should adopt as part of their criteria of whether to grant a firm aid, its size and the industry in which it operates. We considered the change in performance of all the firms that went public between 1972 and 1975 inclusive.

The relationship of profitability to size is familiar ground for economists. Our study differs from others by: a) having as measures of success not only return on assets but the employment the firms generated; b) by being principally concerned with changes in profitability and employment experienced by firms over time rather than with cross-sectional relationships on which previous studies have centred; and c) we have used a very different kind of sample of companies. Whittington(3) employed data on all quoted companies for various periods between 1960 and 1974, whilst Hall and Weiss(4) selected their sample from Fortune's "Top 500" for 1956-62.

Newly quoted companies are of interest because they come most close to new entrepreneurial firms which would be aided if the government acted as a surrogate for the capital market. Flotation may represent the ultimate accolade and may render government aid unnecessary, but these companies would be only one rung up the ladder from those that because of myopia by the capital market would be potential candidates for government assistance.

THE SAMPLE

We have collected data on all 406 companies that went public in 1972-7 inclusive for the year of flotation and, where possible, three year later. After omitting companies that were in finance or non manufacturing, or which were taken over or went out of business or fo some other reason could not provide adequate data (see Appendix) w were left with 94. The mean size of their labour force was 1428 with standard deviation of 3084, the mean value of their assets, £5,554,50 with a standard deviation of £10,116,200 and their average return o assets 24.7%, with a standard deviation of 19.8%.[2] Thus we ar considering the change in performance of companies that at flotation were usually small to medium sized and successful.

THE MODELS

We are principally concerned with whether the size of a firm determine the changes in performance and whether the latter is influenced by th industry in which the firm operates. We have mentioned above som industry-specific reasons for changes in the importance of small firms The success of any firm, of whatever size and however success i defined, may also be dependent on such industry characteristics a market structure and elasticity of demand[3], and where we are employin time series data on changes in these variables. Therefore in ou regressions the SIC, or combinations of close SICs, were introduced a explanatory variables.

We have considered that _a priori_ changes in the profit rates or numbers employed were more likely to be related to percentage changes in size, measured in size of assets or labour force, and that therefore a semi-log specification would be appropriate. However, we have also tested simple linear relationships.

The models we tested were:

1) $\frac{\mathcal{M}}{K_t} = \alpha + B_1 K_t + \epsilon$

2) $\frac{\mathcal{M}}{K_t} = \alpha + B_1 \log_e K_t + \epsilon$

3) $\frac{\mathcal{M}}{K_t} = \alpha + B_1 \log K_t + B_2 \, SIC_{III} \; \ldots \; B_{13} \, SIC_{XIX} + \epsilon$

where:

$\frac{\mathcal{M}}{K_t}$ = return on net assets at flotation

K_t = value of net assets at flotation

$SIC_{III} \ldots SIC_{XIX}$ = SIC constant dummies

These regressions would show whether at flotation size was correlated with return on assets.

4) $\Delta \frac{\mathcal{M}}{K} = \alpha + B_1 K_t + \epsilon$

5) $\Delta \frac{\mathcal{M}}{K} = \alpha + B_1 K_t + B_2 \, SIC_{III} \ldots . B_{13} \, SIC_{XIX} + \epsilon$

6) $\Delta \frac{\mathcal{M}}{K} = \alpha + B_1 \log K_t + \epsilon$

7) $\Delta \frac{\mathcal{M}}{K} = \alpha + B_1 \log K_t + B_2 \, SIC_{III} \ldots . B_{13} \, SIC_{XIX} + \epsilon$

where:

$$\Delta \frac{\mathcal{M}}{K} = \frac{\mathcal{M}}{K_{t+3}} - \frac{\mathcal{M}}{K_t}$$

The results would show the relationship of change in profitability to the size of the firm at flotation.

8) $\Delta \, EM = \alpha + B_1 \, EM_t + \epsilon$

9) $\Delta \, EM = \alpha + B_1 \, EM_t + B_2 \, SIC_{III} \ldots B_{13} \, SIC_{XIX} + \epsilon$

10) $\Delta \, EM = \alpha + B_1 \log EM_t + \epsilon$

11) $\Delta \, EM = \alpha + B_1 \log EM_t + B_2 \, SIC_{III} \ldots B_{13} \, SIC_{XIX} + \epsilon$.

where:

$$\Delta EM = 100 \, \frac{(\text{No of employees}_{t+3} - \text{No of employees}_t)}{\text{No of employees}_t}$$

EM_t = number of employees at flotation.

These would show the relationship between the change in the number employed and the initial size of the labour force.

Dependent Variable \ Independent Variable	Constant	$\frac{Asset_t}{K_t}$ (000)	Log_e Asset	SIC III	SIC V	SIC VII	SIC VIII & IX	SIC XI	SIC XII & VI	SIC XIII	SIC XIV & XV	SIC XVI	SIC XVII	SIC XVIII	SIC XIX	$\bar{R}^2$	D.W.
1) $\frac{Profit}{Asset}\left(\frac{\pi}{K_t}\right)$	0.26188 (11.3)*	-0.0000026 (-1.3)														0.008	1.842
2) $\frac{Profit}{Asset}\left(\frac{\pi}{K_t}\right)$	0.59136 (4.3)*		-0.04385 (-2.5)*													0.0539	1.967
3) $\frac{Profit}{Asset}\left(\frac{\pi}{K_t}\right)$	0.4456 (2.4)*		-0.03866 (-2.09)*	0.03756 (0.64)	0.05175 (0.35)	0.1709 (1.31)	0.07838 (0.62)	0.01756 (0.14)	0.0915 (0.74)	0.00938 (0.07)	0.1678 (1.32)	0.0993 (0.67)	0.146 (1.09)	0.22 (1.75)	0.0205 (0.13)	0.05	2.038
4) % point change of profit rate $\Delta \frac{\pi}{K_t}$	-6.23 (-2.86)*	0.000095 (0.5)														0	2.226
5) % point change of profit rate $\Delta \frac{\pi}{K_t}$	10.0 (0.92)	0.000109 (0.51)		-15.17 (-1.14)	-14.77 (-1.01)	-12.19 (-0.95)	-12.6 (-1.02)	-8.878 (-0.71)	-21.4 (-1.77)	-22.64 (-1.69)	-22.64 (-1.82)	-23.03 (-1.56)	-12.62 (-0.97)	-19.07 (-1.55)	-16.31 (-1.55)	0	2.323
6) % point change of profit rate $\Delta \frac{\pi}{K_t}$	-15.72 (-1.18)		1.276 (0.76)													0	2.26
7) % profit change of profit rate $\Delta \frac{\pi}{K_t}$	-0.834 (-0.04)		1.367 (0.76)	-14.65 (-1.1)	-13.74 (-0.96)	-10.98 (-0.86)	-11.88 (-1.96)	-8.133 (-0.65)	-21.02 (-1.74)	-21.71 (-1.62)	-21.74 (-1.74)	-22.45 (-1.55)	-11.82 (-0.91)	-18.47 (-1.5)	-15.68 (-1.02)	0	2.364

* Significant at 0.05 level

	Dependent Variable \ Independent Variable	Constant	Level of Employment time$_t$ Em_t	Log_e Level of employment	SIC III	SIC V	SIC VII	SIC VIII & IX	SIC XI	SIC XII & VI	SIC XIII	SIC XIV & XV	SIC XVI	SIC XVII	SIC XVIII	SIC XIX	$\bar{R}^2$	D.W.
8)	% Change of Employment Δ EM	33.165 (4.6)*	-0.00404 (-1.9)														0.027	2.185
9)	% Change of Employment Δ EM	15.53 (0.42)	-0.00377 (-1.58)		51.82 (1.13)	12.56 (0.24)	-1.074 (0.025)	41.114 (0.97)	-10.49 (-0.24)	28.68 (0.69)	44.73 (0.98)	-0.648 (-0.02)	-5.958 (-0.12)	36.015 (0.81)	11.67 (0.28)	-12.86 (-0.24)	0.026	2.085
10)	% Change of Employment Δ EM	148.27 (3.52)*		-18.39 (-2.9)*													0.074	2.218
11)	% Change of Employment Δ EM	128.98 (2.29)*		-18.02 (-2.7)*	51.236 (1.16)	4.25 (0.09)	-1.368 (-0.03)	41.23 (1.0)	-8.249 (-0.19)	31.7 (0.79)	39.68 (0.896)	3.35 (0.08)	-3.457 (-0.07)	37.65 (0.87)	5.14 (0.13)	-19.39 (-0.38)	0.058	2.002

* Significant at 0.05 level.

TABLE FIVE

RESULTS

Regressions 1, 2 and 3 above confirm those of Whittington(3) in which the coefficients on net assets were negative and significant at 0.05% but the overall explanatory power of the models was low. Whittington employed industry slope dummies which were negative but usually non-significant. In our results the constant dummies were generally positive but non-significant at the 5% level.

At the time of flotation, therefore there was a weak negative relationship between the size of firms in our sample and their current profitability.

Regressions 4 to 7 would suggest that no relationship exists between the size of a firm at flotation and its subsequent change in profitability. Clearly, though a firm may continue to earn its current rate of profit, there are no grounds for optimism or pessimism about how this will change simply because of its size. Nor are firms in particular industries more likely to experience a change in either direction.

Lastly we consider whether small firms are good horses for the government to back if it wishes to generate employment.Regressions 8-11 show a negative relationship holds but there would not appear to be any industry effects. The overall explanatory power of the model is low. Small firms do generate proportionately bigger increases but the relationship is very weak. Particular industries do not appear to be exceptions to this rule.[4]

SUMMARY AND CONCLUSIONS

1) Census of Production data would suggest an increasingly important small firm sector across the great majority of industries.

2) There would seem little reason to believe, however, that we are observing a dynamic small firm sector and we may be observing the reverse.

3) Neither a firm's size or the industry in which it operates would appear to have very much influence on its profitability at flotation or its subsequent change in either profitability or the number it employs.

FOOTNOTES

1. Measured by either return on assets or by numbers employed.

2. These figures were somewhat distorted by an outlier employing 27,325 workers, the next largest only employing 8503. When this outlier is omitted the figures are mean employment = 1149 (S.D. 1499), mean value of assets 5,021,560 (S.D. 8,744,260) and mean return on assets 24.5% (S.D. 19.7%).

3. This would be suggested by Marcus, M (1969) "Profitability and size of firm: some further evidence", Review of Economics and Statistics, February.

4. It will be noted that we have not corrected for heteroscedasticity. We would expect a priori (confirmed empirically by Samuels F M and Smyth, D J (1968), "Profits, Variability of Profits and Firm Size", Economica, May) that, as large firms might be viewed as portfolios of projects, the variance of their performance would be lower than of small firms without the same opportunity to spread their risks. This would imply that the assumption in OLS of homoscedasticity would be violated. We carried out the test suggested by Park (1966) in "Estimation with heteroscedastic error terms", Econometrica, October and found that the coefficients from

regressing e^2_i and log e^2_i on X_i and log X_i respectively to be non-significant at 0.05% level. In any case as heteroscedasticity produces inefficient parameters this would bias their variances downwards. Where these are high in spite of the presence of heteroscedasticity, this would serve to confirm the lack of any relationship between dependent and explanatory variables.

REFERENCES

1. Birch, D L '*The Job Generation Process*', MIT Programme on Neighbourhood and Regional Change, 1979.

2. Fothergill, S and Gudgin, G 'The Job Generation Process in Britain', *CES Research Series No 32*, 1979.

3. Whittington, G, 'Profitability and the Size of United Kingdom Companies', *Journal of Industrial Economics*, June 1980.

4. Hall, M and Weiss, L 'Firm Size and Profitability', *Review of Economics and Statistics*, August 1967.

APPENDIX

REASONS FOR CHOICE OF SAMPLE OF COMPANIES

(THE DATA WHICH WAS EMPLOYED IN THE REGRESSIONS IN PART II)

Year	Total (excl. overseas)	Finance Companies	Merged	Ceased Trading	Non-manu & Incomplete date	Companies identified with SIC and included in sample
1972	282	104	25	27	68	58
1973	94	32	5	10	21	26
1974	12	3	1	0	2	6
1975	18	8	4	0	2	4
TOTAL	406					94

3 Effects of employment legislation on small firms

AVA WESTRIP
Polytechnic of Central London

INTRODUCTION

A notable feature of the debate in recent years on the job creation potential of small firms has been its focus on the effects of employment legislation. Central to the discussion has been the claim that this legislation has inhibited expansion of employment in the small firm sector. An all-party Parliamentary Select Committee postulated in 1978 that if "each small business could take on one more employee, the unemployment problem would be solved" and called for continuing research into the extent that the Employment Protection Act (EPA) was a deterrent to "small businessmen from taking on additional personnel"(1).

Although a number of bodies have devoted resources to studying the problem, research findings appear to be conflicting. Consequently, public discussion of the issue has become confused and fragmented. Considerable controversy has been stimulated by the legislative measures, resulting latterly in polarised positions, largely (but not exclusively) on party political lines.

So it is now timely to attempt a systematic review and analysis of the issues, examining the findings, methodology, sample sizes and sample construction of a number of surveys relevant to this area of small firms policy. This review, coupled with analysis of official statistics, suggests that recent legislative changes(2) may be an inappropriate method of dealing with the perceived problems. It is further argued that these changes in employment legislation are unlikely to result in any expansion of employment in the small firm sector, may exacerbate the problems of small firm owner-managers, and will almost certainly be to the detriment of small firm employees.

EMPLOYMENT LEGISLATION: A BRIEF BACKGROUND

Traditionally, British governments have been reluctant and cautious in their approach to legislative measures that regulate employers' conduct towards their employees. Early legislation in this area concentrated on checking specific abuses and preventing some of the more flagrant forms of exploitation that accompanied the industrial revolution(3). Historically, health and welfare matters generally seem to have been the paramount interest of legislators(4), but for the most part the employment relationship has remained largely unfettered by statute. Despite dramatic improvements in employment practice since Victorian times, it became clear during the 1960s that the practice of voluntary regulation was no longer adequate to cope with Britain's changing industrial structure.

The first moves away from a reliance on common law were prompted by economic demands, with the social need element acting as leverage for public and political acceptance. Peculiar as it may seem in the present economic environment, the Redundancy Payments Act 1965 was designed to encourage labour shedding(5). This measure and its precursor, the Contracts of Employment Act 1963(6), in fact heralded a new era. A new strategy was taking shape, with the objective of establishing a floor of basic rights for employees.

At the time of the Donovan Report in 1968(7), the law regarded employer and employee as free and equal parties to the employment contract. Thus, an employer was legally entitled to dismiss an employee whenever he wished, provided only that he gave due notice. The employer did not have to offer any reasons, let alone justify them. The Donovan Commission argued that this situation was unsatisfactory because in practice there is usually:

> "no comparison between the consequences for an employer if an employee terminates his contract of employment and those which will ensue for an employee if he is dismissed. In reality people build much of their lives around their jobs. Their incomes and prospects for the future are inevitably founded in the expectation that their jobs will continue. For workers in many situations dismissal is a disaster."(8)

It was against this background that unfair dismissal provisions were introduced initially in the Industrial Relations Act 1971. Thereafter an increasing number of employees qualified for protection against unfair dismissal, mainly by means of reductions in the original qualifying period of two years(9). The initial two-year qualification period appears to have been a somewhat arbitrary threshold, apparently adopted for no better reason than to ensure congruence between estimates of likely case-load and the capacity and resources of the Industrial Tribunal system in the early days(10). Indeed, the Donovan

Commission felt there was "no justification for limiting protection for unfair dismissal to those with at least two years service", since dismissal after a short period "could in some circumstances have a serious effect on an employee's future prospects". The exclusion of small firms from the provisions was similarly rejected by the Commission, since it was considered that tribunals would be able "to take adequate account of the personal factors that inevitably play a larger part in very small undertakings."(11)

Thus the right not to be unfairly dismissed was enshrined in British law; or, more correctly, for the first time the law provided machinery whereby a dismissed employee, with grounds for believing that the reason for termination of the employment was unjust, could seek redress. This becomes an important distnction when the statistics relating to unfair dismissal are discussed later. But firstly we look at another major statute, which laid down additional rights for employees, the EPA(12).

THE EMPLOYMENT PROTECTION ACT

In September 1974, the then Labour Government published its proposals for an extension of individual employment rights. By the end of the consultative period the CBI were reporting widespread employer hostility and the Daily Telegraph claimed that the "heavily biased" bill would "push up industrial costs and hit small companies particularly hard"(13). Hence, even before enactment, the scene was set for the substantial criticism that was to ensue.

Indeed, the EPA was a substantial legislative package, with measures relating to guaranteed pay for workers laid off, maternity pay and maternity leave, time off for redundant workers to look for jobs, revised remedies for unfair dismissal, longer minimum periods of notice and payment of insolvent companies' debts to their former employees(14). Critics of the legislation subsequently suggested that its provisions were inhibiting industrial recovery and thus contributing to the prevailing high levels of unemployment. Employers had become reluctant to engage additional employees, it was claimed, due to the difficulties involved in dismissing them should they prove to be unsuitable or surplus to requirements at a later date. The majority of the individual rights provisions of the EPA came into force on 1 June 1976. Less than one year later, the Policy Studies Institute (PSI) was commissioned(15) to examine some of the consequences of the legislation on manufacturers, and by the Spring of 1978 the Opinion Research Centre (ORC) was conducting interviews with small firms. The major findings of these studies are detailed below.

THE POLICY STUDIES INSTITUTE SURVEY

The PSI examined the practices and policies of a representative sample of 301 private sector manufacturing firms employing between 50 and 5000 employees. The first phase, structured telephone interviews, was followed by more detailed personal interviews within a sub-sample of 36 plants that had experienced a fall in demand but were enjoying a revival at the time of interview. The researchers felt that if employment legislation was having detrimental effects, then it would be most apparent in firms that had experienced fluctuating demand.

In fact, PSI found "very little sign ... that employment protection legislation was inhibiting industrial recovery or contributing to the high level of unemployment by discouraging employers from taking on new people"(16). Where firms with increasing demand for their products were not recruiting, or were recruiting smaller numbers than previously, respondents rarely cited employment legislation as the reason for not increasing their workforce. Increased labour productivity or spare capacity were by far the major reasons spontaneously cited by managers(17).

When subsequently asked directly about the effect of four specific aspects of employment legislation, the unfair dismissal provisions clearly emerged as the most significant in the mind of the respondents (in comparison with redundancy procedures, redundancy pay and guarantee payments for workers on short time or temporarily laid off).

Two important issues arise from these responses. First, as the researchers commented, it was "striking ... that few managers attributed a major impact to any of the items"(18). Secondly, whilst 17% of the respondents considered that unfair dismissal legislation had "a good deal of effect" on their manpower policies, it should not necessarily be inferred from this that the effects were detrimental. Replying to the interviewers' enquiries on the nature of these effects, the most common response was that it had led to the reform of procedures relating to disciplinary action and dismissals, selection and recruitment, induction and training. More attention was paid to recruitment, to ensure that new employees were competent to undertake the job.

At the close of the discussion with the sub-sample respondents, the interviewers posed the question: "Some people argue that the package of employment protection laws has made employers reluctant to recruit because of the increased difficulty of getting rid of people. Would you say that argument makes any sense as far as you are concerned here?"(19). Whilst the question clearly invited agreement, nevertheless two thirds of the respondents said that employment legislation had not inhibited recruitment. The minority who agreed with the proposition generally indicated that the impact was in the direction of additional care in the types of person employed, rather than a reduction in overall numbers.

In their careful analysis of the response, the authors of the report addressed their attention to the particular effects of the legislation on smaller plants. Fifty-four employed less than 200, of which 18 were independent enterprises. Despite the reservations that must be attached to a sub-sample of this size, the report nevertheless shows some interesting results, which are pertinent to the wider debate on the impact of the measures on small firms.

It was found that managers at the smallest plants attributed the least impact to unfair dismissal, whether they were independent or part of a larger organisation(20). Marked differences emerged when dismissal rates were considered: the chances of dismissal appeared to be nearly four times greater in small establishments than in larger organisations. That is, whilst plants employing 1-5000 dismissed one in every 200, smaller plants had dismissed one in every 58 employees during 1977 (only minor differences were noted between independent firms and subsidiaries of larger companies)(21). However, complaints of unfair dismissal showed an opposite trend; the independent small firms employing between 50 and 199 received no complaints. Subsidiary plants of the same size received one complaint for every 25 dismissed; the level of complaint for firms employing between 1000 and 2000 represented one in 10 of those dismissed.

Therefore, where this study isolated the effects of the legislation on small firms, it suggests that generally they fared better than their larger counterparts. The researchers did, however, suggest that the legislation was more unpopular in small firms, whilst having had substantially more influence upon practices of larger firms. Indeed, the researchers, whilst being sympathetic generally to the types of problems that such legislation could create, "unequivocally" rejected "the crude form of criticism" levelled principally by employer interest groups(22).

OPINION RESEARCH CENTRE SURVEY

Before the findings of the PSI research had been published, the ORC conducted an interview programme on behalf of the Department of Employment (DE) for a complementary study on the effects of the legislation on small firms. The randomly selected sample of 301 independent businesses, in five different sectors of industry and commerce, all employed less than 50 employees. Nearly two thirds of the respondents had workforces of 10 or less; these are referred to below as "smaller firms".

The interview schedule, containing over 50 questions, commenced with open questions designed to ascertain whether respondents spontaneously cited employment legislation as a problem. Interviewees were asked whether the size and structure of their labour force had changed and whether business was expanding or contracting. The interviewers then posed increasingly specific questions on the impact of various aspects of employment law. The issue of whether employers had become reluctant to engage additional personnel was raised, both directly and indirectly, at various points during interviews(23).

Respondents attributed little effect to employment law when asked to list the main difficulties experienced in running their business: only 6% mentioned any aspect of the legislation. Issues of much greater concern included financial problems (44%), staff shortages and related problems (35%) and VAT (16%). Smaller firms were <u>less</u> likely to cite legislation as a difficulty(24).

In a general question on the effect of employment legislation, 7% indicated some reluctance to take on more staff, without prompting. Table 1 below summarises the general direction of the responses.

TABLE 1: ORC SURVEY: THE PRINCIPAL FINDINGS

7 said employment legislation was the main difficulty in running their business

22 referred to employment legislation when asked if any government measures had caused difficulties

24 volunteered that they were less likely to take on more staff when asked what effect unfair dismissal legislation had on recruitment

Base 301

Source: DE(25)

However, when asked directly, 24% (71 respondents) said they would have taken on more employees but for the legislation. In view of the apparent discrepancy, the responses given to previous questions by these employers were examined. It seems that the form of the question suggested to respondents an effect that they would not have raised spontaneously. The analysis of responses to earlier questions is shown in Table 2 below.

TABLE 2: ORC SURVEY: ANALYSIS OF PREVIOUS RESPONSES

13 had mentioned employment legislation among their main difficulties

14 had said that no particular government measures caused them difficulty

51 indicated that no government measures related to employment legislation caused them difficulties

29 had indicated that no employment legislation provisions were affecting their business

56 did not find any particular piece of legislation troublesome when confronted with a specific list

Base 71

Source: DE, Research Paper No 6(26)

Indeed, the researchers caution against viewing the response to the prompted question in isolation. It is notable, though, that it is this type of question that has generally been used in the surveys conducted by employer interest groups.

Although unfair dismissal again emerged as the aspect of employment legislation to have had the greatest impact, this resulted in more care in recruitment. In view of the level of criticism directed against the legislation, it is perhaps remarkable that over half the sample (54%)

had no direct experience of any aspect of the legislation. Only 12% said they had experienced and found troublesome at least one item when given a detailed list of current provisions. Although some respondents did feel that employment law created difficulties for firms wishing to reduce their labour force, 63% said it made no difference. The researchers expressed surprise, commenting that the legislation should have made it "at least slightly more difficult to dismiss people"(27).

The study provides evidence that the policies and practices, attitudes and opinions of owner-managers in the sample had been formulated in the light of somwhat imperfect knowledge on employment legislation. No single respondent could correctly answer six straightforward factual questions, only 24% were able to correctly answer a question on the statutory unfair dismissal qualification period, and 21% thought the period was less than the prevailing six months. Moreover, "55% were making no effort to keep up to date" with changes in employment law. "This proportion rose to 64% for the smallest firms (employing ten or less)." In the light of this it is indeed highly questionable whether extension of the unfair dismissal qualification period will have the desired effect of increasing the number of jobs available in the small firm sector.

The researchers concluded that the "results counter the suggestion that the legislation had some massive and widespread effect on small firms"(28). It is therefore somewhat surprising that one year after the preliminary results of this survey were made available by the DE, the Under Secretary of State for Employment was able to proclaim "overwhelming evidence that the present provisions frustrate and unreasonably curtail the creation of jobs"(29).

Further, it was claimed that surveys "undertaken by employers' organisations" apparently showed "convincingly the deterrent effect on employment" arising from the prevailing qualification period(30). In July 1979 the first changes to the EPA were taking place, notably the extension of the unfair dismissal qualification period from 26 to 52 weeks. Our attention therefore now turns to an examination of the surveys that influenced government thinking on the issue.

PRESSURE FOR CHANGE

Employer interest groups had indeed presented a remarkably different picture. Some claimed that 70% or more of small firms have been adversely affected by the legislation(31).

We focus here on studies quoted in Parliament and look firstly at a survey published in July 1979 by the National Federation of Self Employed (NFSE), following a request by a Minister for this organisation's views on changes to the legislation. Its lengthy submission proposed wide-ranging reforms.

Over 70% of NFSE survey respondents claimed that legislation over the last five years had damaged their businesses. Over half those who felt this way (about one third of all those who replied) identified employment protection. Since there was no further examination of the nature of the effects experienced, it does not seem a particularly sound basis for the organisation to claim that "it deters a number of people from taking on employees; it introduces an artificial and unhappy note into relations bewtween small employers and their workers"(32).

The level of impact attributed to legislation generally in this survey was in some ways unsurprising. Given that this organisation, together with a number of others that pressed for reform in this area, have a declared aim to reduce legislative provisions that impinge on the business community, it follows that their membership will consist mainly of those small businessmen who feel most strongly that government action reduces their freedom. This argument must apply with even more force to those members who take the time and trouble to actually complete a questionnaire.

It was, in fact, suggested in a House of Lords debate that this survey had more validity than the PSI and ORC studies, simply because it involved more respondents (1000)(33). However, this ignores the important factor that the PSI and ORC samples were constructed on rigorous research principles to be representative of the industries and size categories under study. It is perhaps more salient to point out in relation to the NFSE survey that since 98% of the membership failed to respond, it was probably not even representative of this organisation's subscribers, let alone small firms in general.

Moreover, examination of a number of questionnaires shows a tendency for certain interest groups to utilise somewhat leading questions, and thereby perhaps suggest to recipients issues which they would not otherwise have considered.

For example, one questionnaire entitled "Employment Protection or Prevention", requested "ammunition" for their spokesmen. Respondents were informed that the "provisions of the Employment Protection Act have been mentioned as an important reason why small firms do not take on more workers. Please tell us how significant it is to your business in terms of jobs now and your plans for the next couple of years". Over 800 people responded; 80% agreed with the implicit suggestion(34). This organisation has a strong political base; it therefore seems possible that respondents were expressing general antipathy towards the policies of the incumbent Labour Government.

Although the response rate to this survey was probably higher than some others, it was not possible to clearly define the total survey population with any certainty. Nor is any information available on the types or size of participating firms. In view of these reservations, it is difficult to regard the results as a sufficiently firm basis for legislative change.

Both the PSI and ORC studies showed that objective assessment of the responses was facilitated by additional information, such as the level of product demand, changes in the structure of the firm's labour force, or whether the respondents understood the legislation. Employers' associations have generally relied on self-administered questionnaires, in which there is obviously less scope for examining issues in the same depth. In the event, it was found that little attempt was made to endeavour to examine any other factor than whether the respondent was prepared to say that the legislation was detrimental. A recent report by the Labour Relations Agency (Northern Ireland's equivalent of the Advisory, Conciliation and Arbitration Service) on the employment problems of small manufacturing firms pointed to a dichotomy:

> "Several of the owner/managers interviewed expressed strong views about new employment legislation and argued that it acted as a constraint upon employment ... it is significant to note that some of those who argued this point had in fact increased their workforce during the period employment legislation has been in force."(35)

One survey which did collect some information on other constraints failed to link the various factors in its analysis. The primary aim of the Engineering Employers' Federation survey seems to have been to collect evidence that the legislation had inhibited employment. The questionnaire entitlted "Impact on Labour Market of Recent Employment Legislation" asked whether expansion of employment had been restricted:

> "If, in the period since the beginning of 1975, general economic and business conditions had been more favourable and/or taxation lighter and/or employment legislation less burdensone, do you consider that your company would now be employing a larger number of employees? YES/NO."

Respondents answering "no" were instructed to turn to the end of the document to answer a question on Temporary Employment Subsidies; thus no attempt was made to elicit views from these companies. Only affirmative responses were included in the analysis, thereby excluding the 20% or so respondents that were unable to agree with the above statement. Difficult economic conditions were by far the most important factor limiting expansion; lack of orders, shortage of skilled labour and inflation featured most prominently (categories which were, predictably, prompted).

Although some surveys asked respondents to estimate the number of people they would have taken on but for the legislation, it seems to produce a rather meaningless figure, unless respondents are able to demonstrate sufficient demand for their goods or services, that the required labour would actually have been available or that they had sufficient working capital to sustain such expansion. A postal survey, conducted by Birmingham Chamber of Industry and Commerce, did in fact concentrate on this aspect, simply asking its membership to estimate the number of jobs not created or filled during that year "as a direct result of the existing employment legislation". The survey report makes the somewhat dramatic claim that on average 9.4 job opportunities per firm have been lost as a direct result of the legislation. But only 5% of the membership responded; and nearly half of those that produced estimates of "lost" jobs said that "in effect, the employment legislation had not had such a direct effect on their recruitment/employment policies". Respondents were also given a list of employment law provisions and asked to rank these in order of importance. Ministers were subsequently urged to amend the legislation in the light of the evidence presented in this report.

It is an essential part of the function of a pressure group to obtain publicity for its view; but to suppose that the results of such surveys are impartial or comparable with the standards of independent research focussing on randomly selected samples, is clearly unrealistic. Nearly 10 years ago, the Bolton Committee Report on small firms similarly identified a marked disparity between evidence submitted by employers' associations and the results of independent research commissioned by the Committee. The report pointed to "a large measure of straightforward political prejudice against the Labour Government at that time"(36). Indeed, there are indications in the material collected from the orgaisations that have pressed for reform of employment legislation that the issue has generally been used as a platform for complaint against a government regarded as being unsympathetic to private enterprise. Moreover, it appears that some small business pressure groups may have stimulated antagonism towards the measures, by disseminating misleading or inaccurate information(37) both to their members and through the national press. On a similar theme, one researcher has commented:

> "Much of the press coverage gives the impression that unfair dismissal legislation is very restrictive and it may be that criticism and anxiety expressed by small employers arise from misunderstanding or ignorance of the legislative provisions. if this is the case, changing them ... will make little difference to the employer while diminishing the rights of employees."(38)

RECENT CHANGES

Extensive changes in employment legislation have been enacted since the present government took office. Firstly, by means of Variation Orders, the unfair dismissal qualification period was extended from 26 to 52 weeks and the statutory consultation period on redundancies involving between 10 and 99 workers reduced from 60 to 30 days. Secondly, the Employment Act (1980) contained changes directed specifically at small firms. New recruits to firms employing 20 or less now do not have the right of complaint against unfair dismissal until they have worked for the firm continuously for two years.

Industrial tribunals will be specifically required to take into account the size and administrative resources of the employer and the onus of proof is to be "neutral". The Act permits fixed term contracts of one year's duration, waiving unfair dismissal rights on expiry. Firms with five employees or less finding it "not reasonably practicable" to reinstate a woman after maternity leave will be relieved of the obligation.

Although the changes have variously been described as "watery amendments" and "a cosmetic approach"(39), the package in fact represents a substantial negative shift in the protection afforded to employees. Throughout the lengthy debates on these issues the government have continued to maintain that new employment opportunities will be created:

> "our theme is that new employment can, most hopefully, be looked for from the small business sector. Our theme is that the employment protection legislation acts as a block on that generation."(40)

A review of the Parliamentary debates indicates several important issues. Firstly, it was noticeable that the government arguments, at least in some respects, appeared to closely mirror the approach advocated by small business pressure groups. Secondly, there was clearly confusion over the apparently conflicting survey findings. Moreover, there were indications that the methodological shortcomings of the pressure group surveys were regarded as unimportant. Since the research sponsored by the DE could not be disregarded, a somewhat selective approach was taken. It will be recalled from the earlier review of the ORC survey that it was not until the researchers specifically prompted the notion that the legislation might be inhibiting expansion of employment that any significant affirmative response was forthcoming. Rather than viewing the findings in their totality, this one question (which represents one end of a broad spectrum) was held to be the key to future developments:

"As it was a thorough poll, various questions were asked in differing order. But one question received an answer from 24 per cent of the respondents that they would have taken on more employees but for the legislation ... If only 12 per cent - let alone 24 per cent - of such employers regard the present employment legislation as putting up a barrier to their taking on more people, its removal could lead to higher employment."(41)

Thus the wider implications of the ORC study were ignored in favour of a question that reflected pressure group orthodoxy, despite the ambiguity of respondents highlighted in the researchers' careful analysis. To suggest that those who have agreed with a leading question will expand their labour force once changes in employment legislation are enacted seems somewhat naive, particularly if, as in the case of the ORC respondents, they perceive financial problems and staff shortages as dominant problems.

Since analysis of survey data suggests doubt must attach to the claim that the legislation has discouraged recruitment, our attention is now turned to unfair dismissal statistics to ascertain whether this supports the assertion that the provisions "bear over-harshly ... on small businesses"(42).

UNFAIR DISMISSAL STATISTICS

As unfair dismissal legislation appears to have caused the greatest concern, statistics on the incidence of complaints and their outcomes are reviewed below. The number of registered complaints rose rapidly as the qualification period was reduced, from under 10,000 in 1973 and stabilising at around 38,000 a year with the qualification period of six months. Given the estimate of at least 1.25m job terminations each year(43), the proportion alleging unfair dismissal seems noticeably low. Only a minority of these complaints go forward to a tribunal hearing. Nearly two thirds are dealt with by conciliation and an increasing proportion (nearly half) are withdrawn by the applicant. In 1978 the tribunals heard less than 12,000 cases and the employer was judged to have acted unfairly in just 28% of these cases(44).

Almost a quarter of these complaints involved firms employing less than 20 employees(45). The DE have suggested that small establishments are over-represented in the statistics, by drawing comparisons with Census of Employment data on the number of employees working in smaller workplaces(46). Certain reservations must attach to this approach since it implies an assumption that dismissal is always employee initiated.

Since the act of dismissal represents the interaction of two distinct forms of benaviour (the behaviour of the employee and an employer's response to that behaviour), it would seem necessary also to consider the number of firms. On this basis, and concentrating on firms employing less than 20, it would appear that each year a complaint is made against less than one in every hundred firms. It is also noticeable that over the whole period of unfair dismissal legislation the distribution of unfair dismissal complaints between firms of differing sizes has altered very little(47).

However, since it seems to be widely accepted that small firms are over-represented, two questions need to be asked. Why should this be so and is the system biased against small firms? These issues are considered in turn.

Golby and Johns in their research report for the Bolton Committee(48) suggested that the underlying motivation for many owner-managers was the need to "attain and preserve independence", with personal satisfaction ranking as a high priority, often at the expense of rationality. Thus where the desire for autonomy and self esteem are dominant goals, he tends to adopt a highly personalised style of management, sometimes paternalistic, often autocratic. Resistant to delegating decision-making, he is less likely to consult with colleagues or discuss the perceived problems with the employee before taking the decision to dismiss. Since personal characteristics of employees often appear more important to the owner-manager than skill level, previous training or formal qualifications, any perceived deterioration is unlikely to be tolerated. Priding himself on an informal and flexible form of management, the owner-manager may be inconsistent in the standards he applies, not only to different individuals but with the same employee over a period of time. In short, personnel management in the small firm is likely to be very different to the approach adopted in larger concerns, with a far greater likelihood of the owner-manager dismissing at a whim. In fact, there are many reasons to suggest that smaller firms will feature more frequently in the statistics than the percentage of people they employ would at first lead one to expect.

Small firms are significantly less likely to have established disciplinary and dismissal procedures, partly due to the belief that these would lead to an excessive formalisation of relationships(49). Although recent research suggests that as many as 60% of firms employing less than 20 claim to have such procedures(50) it seems that these respondents, having experienced an unfair dismissal complaint, may have overstated the position. The ACAS Code of Practice, which lays down guidelines for the handling of disciplinary and dismissal matters(51), had been obtained by 16% of the ORC respondents, but only 5% claimed to have made use of it. Relatively few had obtained any of the DE's explanatory leaflets(52). Similarly, many small firms do not issue 'contracts' of employment(53) or keep written records of personnel matters. Hence, many owner-managers do not understand the legislation or how to adapt their management practices to nullify any possible adverse effects. Indeed, there are indications that many simply ignore the implications of the legislation until faced with an unfair dismissal claim(54).

Critics claim that tribunals deal over-harshly with small firms. However, whilst there seems to be every indication that small firms could well have more problems than the larger firm, tribunals in the past have been sympathetic to the difference between small and large firms(55) and do not impose their own standards, but concentrate on what "is reasonable in the circumstances"(56). Despite this, there are marked differences in the success rate of claims. An analysis of a 10% representative sample of 1978 unfair dismissal cases indicated that whilst firms employing over 1000 won over 80% of their cases, firms with less than 50 employees won around 60%(57). Indeed, perhaps one of the most surprising indications in these figures is how few applicants dismissed from large firms have their cases upheld by a tribunal. Small firms are more likely than large to settle at conciliation. Thus, overall about 54% of applicants from firms employing less than 20 received a remedy from their former employers (whether at conciliation or at a tribunal hearing) compared with the average rate of 45%(58).

Though small firm employees <u>are</u> more likely to receive a remedy as a result of a complaint of unfair dismissal, comparisons may be misleading, since many larger firms have relatively sophisticated internal appeals procedures to deal speedily and promptly with any dispute over a dismissal decision. It is difficult to accept on the basis of these figures that there is excessive bias against small firms, unless we concede the implied suggestion that the owner-manager is invariably fair in his behaviour.

Although it appears that the number of unfair dismissal complaints will reduce as a result of the recent changes and that employees' complaints are less likely to be upheld by the tribunals, it is doubtful whether any other benefit will accrue(59).

Where small firms have reformed their recruitment and disciplinary procedures as a result of the legislation, this has generally been beneficial to both employers and employees. As the Labour Relations Agency have pointed out:

> "The introduction of adequate procedures assist the firm in controlling absenteeism, lateness and general disciplinary matters and offer benefits to both employer and employee in ensuring fairness and consistency in the application of disciplinary action. The introduction of such procedures need not lead to excessive formalisation of relationships as feared by some owner/managers - those firms which had introduced procedures did not claim any deterioration in relationships."(60)

Thus, the benefits which have gradually begun to accrue in the small firm sector as a result of the legislation may be lost as a result of recent amendments.

Perhaps more importantly, the Employment Act seems to have made individual rights legislation more complex, with greater scope for misunderstanding(61). Small businessmen already have many misconceptions about employment law, and unless considerable effort is made to effectively communicate the changes, they may present more actual or perceived problems than have previously been experienced. Moreover, since the changes provide less incentive than formerly for the introduction of disciplinary procedures, they could act as a spur to the greater unionisation in the small firm sector, a move unlikely to be welcomeed by many owner-managers.

SMALL FIRM WORKERS

Small firms are often the most vulnerable to the economic and competitive pressures of a modern economy, and this is particularly true during periods of economic recession or inflation. Despite the flexibility that typifies the sector, many small businesses do not have the resources to survive the difficult times unscathed. It follows that their employees are in an exposed situation when downturns in the economy are imminent, whether this is a short term or further reaching phenomenon. Thus many small firm workers have less security of employment generally; this is particularly marked in the lowest paying sectors, which are often subject to fluctuating demand.

Although the Bolton Report(62) suggested that generally small firms had low labour turnover levels, there appears to be no empirical data in the report to support the assertion. Rather, the reverse appears to be true. official statistics indicate that sectors with the highest proportions of small firms have markedly higher numbers of employees with short periods of service. Across the economy as a whole, about 11% of adult employees have less than one year's service with their current employer. More than a quarter of full-time adult males and over a third of adult females have less than two years' service, but the proportions rise to 50% of males and nearly half for female employees in sectors dominated by small firms(63).

Similarly, recent research focussing on workers in printing and electronics firms found that 45% of the small firm workers studied had been with their current employer for less than a year, compared with 27% in large firms in the same industries and locality. Moreover, examination of the employment patterns of the employees suggested that the small firm workers had relatively unstable work histories - mainly short periods of service in small firms. The rigidity of large firm employment policies suggests that these workers would be excluded from the better pay, conditions and employment protection offered by larger firms, due to their work histories, lower skill levels and frequent absence of formal qualifications. Thus, for many, employment in a small firm is not a free choice, but the result of a variety of external pressures pushing them towards the marginal enterprise(65).

Weakening employment protection legislation in small firms therefore appears to add to the wider matrix of labour market disadvantage faced by a vulnerable, often low paid, group of workers.

The labour instability levels discussed above, in fact point to a problem that in practical terms appears to be far greater than the alleged difficulties arising from employment legislation.

RECRUITMENT AND LABOUR TURNOVER PROBLEMS

A more serious problem for many small firms in the field of employment appears to centre on the difficulties encountered in attracting and retaining the right kind of employee. Bolton Committee Research Reports(65) pointed to this nearly 10 years ago, and the difficulties do not appear to have diminished. Similarly, the respondents in the ORC study were substantially more likely to spontaneously raise a problem of this nature than to mention employment legislation as a difficulty. In short, many small firms appear to find it difficult to compete for labour in a modern economy.

Ironically, around the same time as the government announced its major proposals for reform of employment legislation, three prominent employer interest groups published survey findings on the difficulties being experienced with staff shortages, especially in small firms(66).

The labour turnover levels discussed above highlight two other important issues. Firstly, many employers are continuing to recruit to make up for wastage. Secondly, the short periods of service indicate that many small firm employees will not qualify in future to complain of unfair dismissal. It is noticeable that the sectors that in the past have accounted for nearly half of unfair dismissal complaints - distributive trades, miscellaneous services and construction (sectors with large numbers of small firms) - have a markedly higher incidence of employees with less than two years service.

SUMMARY AND CONCLUSIONS

Modern employment legislation in the UK dates back to the mid 1960s. One of the most important innovations has been the change from the minimal rights allowed under common law concerning dismissal from employment, to the statutory right not to be unfairly dismissed. Thus the duty was imposed upon employers to ensure that there was just cause for any dismissal. Individual rights legislation was further extended by the EPA 1975, a statute which stimulated considerable controversy. Critics claimed that the legislation inhibited expansion of employment in the small firm sector. Yet the aspect which has been the subject of the greatest criticism, the unfair dismissal provisions, in fact was first introduced in the Industrial Relations Act 1971. As a result of the mounting criticism of the measures and pressure for change, the legislation has recently been substantially modified. Workers in small firms will have fewer rights, which represents a move away from the original intention to give all employees equal protection under the law. It has been argued that new employment opportunities will derive from changes in unfair dismissal legislation. However, analysis of the research and statistics which appear to have been utilised in formulation of policy leaves some doubt that this end will be achieved.

Surveys conducted by employer interest groups seem to be strangely at odds with those conducted by independent research organisations, since the former suggest widespread and debilitating effects which have not been borne out by the latter. Closer inspection reveals that methodological differences provide not only the explanatory key, but indicate which category has the greater validity. To illustrate these points, this paper has reviewed two independent studies and four employer interest group surveys, and has drawn on other research to support the tentative conclusions presented here.

The surveys conducted by the PSI and the ORC focussed on randomly selected samples, designed to be broadly representative of the populations under study. Employers' organisations on the other hand relied mainly on the attitudes and opinions of their own members. The actions of the latter in joining the organisation probably sets them apart from other businessmen, especially where it is an association with a declared hostility towards legislation. As these surveys generally had low response rates, it would appear that the samples were doubly self-selected, thus reflecting the views of those that felt most strongly about the subject.

Yet it is not only the nature of the samples which suggest that extreme caution should be exercised in interpreting the results of these surveys. The ORC survey indicated the importance of the phraseology of questions, finding that little impact was attributed to the legislation until the notion that it might be inhibiting recruitment was prompted. Our analysis suggests that to a greater or lesser extent all the employer interest groups used leading questions, seemingly indicating the type of replies that were required. Affirmative answers to a question such as "would you have employed more people but for the legislation?" provide no guarantee that expansion of employment will automatically ensue when the legislation is reformed. Thus, employer interest group surveys do not appear to provide a sound basis for legislative change. Independent research reveals that the legislation appears to have had a relatively minor impact, although it cannot be denied that many small businessmen express hostility towards it. This antagonism appears to reflect two different aspects of a seemingly single problem. Clear differentiation is needed here since only one of these can be alleviated effectively by policy measures. Firstly, small businessmen appear to have a low level of understanding of the legislation and perceive it as being unnecessarily restrictive. Since in reality all that the legislation requires is a minimum standard of management behaviour towards employees, there is a clear need for an educative programme to reduce this anxiety. Whilst there is a strong case for suggesting that such a programme should have preceded any legislative change, it becomes even more necessary if the recent reforms are to have any effect at all. Secondly, many owner-managers appear to regard the legislation as a challenge to management prerogatives, thus exhibiting an ideological resistance to the principles that underline the legislation. Hence there is a clash between the strong belief of many small businessmen in their right to manage their business free from outside interference, and the demands of a workforce which has expectations beyond being a mere factor of production. Whilst present policy appears to have in large measure reflected an ideological demand, it is questionable whether this will have any significant impact on levels of employment in the individual firm or across the small firm sector as a whole.

REFERENCES

1. Thirteenth Report from the Expenditure Committee, People and Work, Prospects for Jobs and Training, HMSO, 1978, pp 50 and 80.

2. Unfair Dismissal (Variation of Qualifying Period) Order 1979; Employment Protection (Handling of Redundancies) Variation Order 1979; Employment Act 1980 and Industrial Tribunals (Rules of Procedure) Regulations 1980. The alterations in individual rights legislation are summarised later under the heading "Changes".

3. eg. Ten Hours Act 1847, limiting child labour in textile factories; 1840 and 1875 measures abolishing the practice of child chimneysweeps ('climbing boys'); Truck Act 1831, outlawing "The company shop"; Trade Boards Act 1909, intended to protect workers in the "Sweated trades" by statutory regulation of their pay. Trade Boards are now called Wages Councils.

4. Clegg, H A, The System of Industrial Relations in Great Britain, 3rd ed, Blackwell, 1976, Chapter 9, The State in Industrial Relations: The Traditional Pattern, pp 334-346.

5. Daniel, W W and Stilgoe, E, The Impact of Employment Protection Laws, Policy Studies Institute, June 1978, p 11.

6. Whitehead, E and Bronkhurst, R, The Real Cost of Dismissal, Incomes Data Services and The Financial Times, 1979, Part 2, Parliament's Rules and Penalties, p 17.

7. Royal Commission on Trade Unions and Employers' Associations 1965-1968, Cmnd 3623, HMSO, 1968, The Report is usually referred to as The Donovan Report after the name of the Commission's Chairman.

8. ibid, Chapter IX, Safeguards for Employees against Unfair Dismissal, para 526 (see also para 521).

9. Reductions in unfair dismissal qualification period: September 1974: continuous service qualification reduced from 104 to 52 weeks; March 1975: reduced to 26 weeks; October 1976: small firms exclusion removed, ie. firms with less than 4 workers no longer exempted; February 1977: protection extended to some part-time workers.

10. Clark, G de N, Remedies for Unjust Dismissal, Proposals for Legislation, PEP, June 1970, p 32, see also Lewis, R, Davies, P and Wedderburn, B, Industrial Relations Law and the Conservative Government, Fabian Society, 1979, p 43.

11. Donovan Report, op cit, Paras 555 and 556.

12. Note: other important aspects of modern employment legislation have been excluded from this brief summary since generally they have attracted less criticism than the Employment Protection Act. eg. Equal Pay Act 1970; Contracts of Employment Act 1972; Health and Safety at Work Act 1974; Race Relations Act 1976; Trade Union and Labour Relations Act 1974 and Amendment Act 1976.

13. The Daily Telegraph, "CBI ready for clash on 'biased' employment Bill", 2 December 1974, p 14. Also Financial Times, 19 November 1974, "Small companies ... are horrified at the potential cost of the proposed Bill".

14. Department of Employment Gazette, April 1976, p 385.

15. Department of Employment and Manpower Services Commission.

16. Daniel and Stilgoe, PSI, op cit, p 77.

17. ibid, pp 64-69.

18. ibid, p 43.

19. ibid, p 70.

20. ibid, p 45.

21. ibid, p 62.

22. ibid, p 77.

23. Clifton, R and Tatton-Brown, C, Impact of Employment Legislation on Small Firms, Research Paper No 6, Department of Employment, 1979. Referred to in the text as the Opinion Research Centre (ORC) Survey.

24. ibid, pp 8-11.

25. Department of Employment Press Notice, "Impact of Employment Legislation on Small Firms", August 1978.

26. Clifton and Tatton-Brown, op cit, p 22.

27. ibid, p 23.

28. ibid, p 33.

29. House of Commons Official Report, Parliamentary Debates, Hansard, Vol 971, No 46, 25 July 1979, Col 523 (The Under Secretary of State for Employment, Mr Patrick Mayhew).

30. ibid, Col 531.

31. eg. EEF News, December 1978. The Guardian,Small Business Guardian, "Frightening Protection for Workers", 21 January 1978, p 17.

32. First Voice, Vol 3, No 7, July 1979, pp 6-7. Although the NFSE Small Businss Opinion Survey 1979 was not primarily concerned with employment law, it appears to have been offered as evidence, being published with the Federation's proposals for extensive changes in the legislation.

33. House of Lords Official Report, Parliamentary Debates, Hansard, Vol 401, No 33, 25 July 1979, Cols 1962 and 1975 (Lord Spens).

34. Preliminary results of the Small Business Bureau Survey were reported in The Guardian, 21 January 1978, op cit. A summary of the completed survey was reported in Small Business, "Employment Laws are preventing jobs!", July 1978, p 12.

35. Labour Relations Agency, A Report on the Industrial Relations and Employment Problems of Small anufacturing Firms, Occasional Paper No 5, December 1979, p 5 (Unfair dismissal legislation did not apply in Northern Ireland until 1976).

36. Small Firms, Report of the Committee of Inquiry on Small Firms, Cmnd 4811, HMSO, 1971, Generally known as The Bolton Report, Para 9.3.

37. eg. Slow to Hire, Quick to Fire: A Warning to Employers about Recent Employment Legislation, Counterattack, November 1976. Small Business, "Unfair Dismissal - The ABC of New Employment Awards", April 1978. National Federation of Self-Employed, The End of the ACAS Blackmail Gang, June 1978.

38. Dickens, L, Hart, M, Jones, M and Weekes, B, A Response to the Government Working papers on Amendments to Employment Protection Legislation, Discussion Paper, Industrial Relations Research Unit of the Social Science Research Council, University of Warwick, November 1979, Section 1, p 3.

39. The Guardian, Guardian Small Business Letters, 19 October 1979. Business Law Review, Vol 1, No 1, Employment Law: A Cosmetic Approach, January 1980, pp 9-11.

40. House of Commons Official Report, Standing Committee A, Employment Bill, Eighteenth Sitting, 6 March 1980, Col 954.

41. ibid, Twelfth Sitting, 21 February 1980, Col 634.

42. Department of Employment Gazette, Employment Protection Legislation, Working Paper on Proposed Amendments, September 1979.

43. Personnel Management, August 1978, p 11. Published estimates of dismissals per annum vary widely and one source suggests a figure of 3 million (see data cited by Lewis, P, 'Employment protection: a preliminary assessment', Industrial Relations Journal, Vol 12, No 2, March/April 1981, pp 19-29.

44. Department of Employment Gazette, Unfair Dismissal cases in 1978, September 1979, pp 866-867. 1979 statistics show a similar pattern, Employment Gazette, Unfair Dismissal Cases in 1979, February 1981, p 82.

45. Department of Employment published and unpublished statistics, cited in Westrip, A, 'An investigation of the impact of employment protection laws on the small firm, with special reference to unfair dismissal legislation', Small Business Unit, Polytechnic of Central London, September 1979.

46. Department of Employment Gazette, June 1975, p 532.

47. Westrip, op cit.

48. Golby, C W and Johns, G, Attitude and Motivation, Committee of Inquiry on Small Firms, Research Report No 7, HMSO, 1971. Golby and Johns' report can be criticised for presenting a stereotype that does not reflect differences between owner-managers and differences in motivation over time. For a broader analysis see Stanworth, M J K and Curran, J, Management Motivation in the Smaller Business, Gower, 1973 and Stanworth and Curran, Growth and the Small Firm - An Alternative View, Journal of Management Studies, Vol 13, No 2, May 1976, pp 95-110.

49. Labour Relations Agency, op cit, p 4.

50. Dickens et al, op cit, p 6 (IRRU survey of 1013 randomly selected employers who were party to an unfair dismissal application registered between October 1976 and September 1977).

51. Advisory, Conciliation and Arbitration Service, Code of Practice 1, Disciplinary practice and procedures in employment, HMSO.

52. Clifton and Tatton-Brown, op cit, pp 25-28.

53. Labour Relations Agency, op cit. Employers Monitor, Eighth Edition (Employers Protection Insurance Service Ltd, June 1979). Employers are required to provide a written statement of the main terms and conditions of employment (within a prescribed period, depending on the number of hours worked per week) which should include a note specifying any disciplinary rules and any procedures that will be followed in the event of the employer taking any disciplinary or dismissal action against the employee. This statement is often referred to as a 'contract' of employment.

54. Labour Relations Agency, op cit.

55. Dickens et al, op cit, pp 17-18.

56. Croner's Reference Book for Employers, February 1979, p 146.

57. Westrip, op cit.

58. The term "remedy" means broadly re-engagement or financial compensation.

59. During the period 1 October 1979 to the end of April 1980, registered unfair dismissal complaints fell by 26%, Employment Gazette, July 1980, p 753. However, the overall difference between comparison of these two years suggests a sharp reversal of the decline in registrations, occurring from July 1980 onwards. This trend appears to reflect the rapidly increasing level of unemployment (seasonablly unadjusted, excluding school leavers) during the second half of 1980. For relevant statistical data see House of Commons Official Report, Parliamentary Debates, Hansard, Vol 999, No 49, 17 February 1980, written answers, Cols 91-92, Employment Gazette, January 1981, p 522.

60. Labour Relations Agency, op cit, p 9.

61. For expansion of this point see Westrip, A, The Guardian, Small Business Guardian, "New controls govern 'unfair' dismissals", 16 January 1981, p 16.

62. The Bolton Report, op cit, Para 2.40.

63. New Earnings Survey 1979, Analyses by length of service, tables 167-169, Department of Employment, March 1980.

64. Curran, J and Stanworth, M J K, Self-selection and the Small Firm Worker - A Critique and An Alternative View, Sociology, Vol 13, No 3, September 1979, pp 427-444. See also by the same authors - Some Reasons Why Small is not always Beautiful, New Society, 14 December 1978.

65. Merrett Cyriax Associates, Dynamics of Small Firms, Committee of Enquiry on Small Firms, Research Report No 12, HMSO, 1971, pp 2 and 20. Golby and Johns, op cit. The study by Wilson in this collection also points to labour shortages as a major problem.

66. The Guardian, Small Business Guardian, "The Problems of Finding Skilled Staff", 21 September 1979, p 20, reporting on "The Employment Paradox in Smaller Firms", Association of Independent Businesses, October 1979. The Financial Times, "Companies growth hit by skills shortage", 1 October 1979. The Financial Times, "Shortage of Skilled Labour in Midlands", 7 October 1979, p 7.

4 Large firm assistance to small firms

VICKI SARGENT
London Enterprise Agency

WHY DO LARGE FIRMS WANT TO HELP SMALL FIRMS?

A growing number of Britain's major companies are now allocating resources to programmes for fostering new enterprise outside the company through small firms. The pioneering efforts made in this field by Pilkingtons in St Helens, By ICI and by British Steel, are now being taken up by other larger firms.

These activities might at first sight seem opposed to the real commercial ends of these large companies, and the motives behind them need explaining. A key motive arises from their increased sensitivity to the contribution they have made to long-term unemployment, through investment in new technology or transfer of manufacturing activities overseas. The current recession, which has seen such a shakeout in large manufacturing industry, has naturally played increasingly on this sensitivity.

Most of the early initiatives to help foster small business were taken by large firms which were dominant employers in particular communities, and consequently felt committed to making efforts to compensate that community when cutting back on employment opportunities themselves. The best known example is Pilkington Brothers who, in 1979, announced a major investment programme which would result ultimately in the loss of 2800 jobs - a significant disruption for a small community like St Helens, largely dependent on its glass industry. In response to this, Pilkingtons undertook a series of measures to encourage the creation of new enterprises in the area, centred around the St Helens Trust.

The decimation of areas by the closure of one dominant source of employment was also behind the creation of British Steel (Industries) Limited by British Steel Corporation (BSC). It was closures in the Clyde and Ebbw Vale areas in 1975 that prompted BSC to set up this vehicle through which resources could be made available to encourage new industries to locate there.

The activities of ICI in helping small businesses originated from an appreciation of the problems caused by a lack of structural balance in local economies, particularly noticeable in the North West and North East where ICI is a substantial employer. Much impetus has been given to these activities as a result of ICI's own need to cut employment levels sharply in order to remain viable. The scale of these cuts can be illustrated by a few figures.

Average UK employment in ICI fell from 92,500 in 1978 to 89,000 in 1979 and 76,000 in 1981. These figures reflect problems in the fibres, plastics and organics divisions, accentuated by the economic recession. ICI does not expect that general economic recovery in the UK will bring any reversal of that trend. Hence the special initiatives taken by them to encourage self-employment and foster small business growth.

These initiatives by ICI, Pilkingtons and BSC arose largely from their assumption of some responsibility for the effects on employment in local areas of their own corporate policies. A slightly wider approach which has drawn many large companies into the 'large firm/small firm movement' is attributable to growing concern amongst industrialists about the economic and social effects of large-scale unemployment and the benefits of a more vibrant small firm sector. Large companies themselves are, at best, not increasing employment and, at worst, are pruning workforces heavily. This recession in particular is being used to cut manning levels as much as possible, and investment in the upturn is most likely to be in labour-saving new technology.

Because there are not obvious alternative sources of employment (as, in the sixties, for example, government was) to take up these jobs, large firms are beginning to look at the possibilities for creating new jobs outside their firms. The best known expression of this idea was given by a former chairman of Shell in his 1977 Ashridge Lecture, "More Jobs - A small cure for a big problem"(1). He pointed out that:

> "Industry cannot just opt out of society's problems, particularly those that press on the local community where it operates ... I believe that large-scale industry, whilst remaining efficient and profitable (which is of course its overriding duty), also has a duty to help in its own localities."

While the first initiatives by large firms acting on their own or in groups arose spontaneously and independently, efforts are now being made to coordinate activities and encourage other large firms to become involved. These efforts are being made both by the Department of

Environment and by the Pilkington Committee, a working group of senior representatives from major companies chaired by Sir Alistair Pilkington.

CAN SMALL FIRMS DO IT?

Given this emerging sense of responsibility for employment and the health of the economy, why have large firms (like the government) chosen to concentrate efforts on small firms? If assisted, can small firms produce the economic 'goods' - not just in the form of jobs, but also in innovation, efficiency and economic growth - which will create jobs in the future?

The publication in 1979 of the Birch Report(2) had unfortunate consequences on the quality and constructiveness of the debate about the small firm support policies pursued in the private and public sectors. Birch's report indicated that in the US in the years between 1969 and 1976, firms with 20 employees or less generated 66% of net employment. The effect of this report in England was that while politicians seized upon it as justification for putting resources into small firms, academics concentrated on disputing Birch's figures and producing other figures showing that in the UK, historically, small firms have not created as many jobs as larger firms.

The irrelevance of this approach is surely obvious: what we need to know is the response of different sizes of firms to practicable policies that might be applied to them. But equally, should we really be trying to justify a small firms policy in terms of short-term job creation? There are certainly more effective ways of creating jobs in the short term than backing small firms - spending more on defence, or construction for instance. But these policies are not necessarily sustainable, economically or politically.

A small firms policy should not pretend to be a panacea for unemployment, although in the longer term, by making the birth and growth of new firms and the expansion of existing small firms easier and more efficient, it will increase the pool from which the relatively small number of successful businesses rise.

Thankfully, there is now recognition within government circles that small firms have more to contribute to the economic fabric of the country than jobs. This was revealed in a speech by Mrs Thatcher at the launch of the government's new Business Opportunities Programme in May 1981, when she indicated that a small firms policy was not solely for the purpose of creating jobs in manufacturing industry.

Further criticism of small firm policies has been on the grounds that small units of production are necessarily inefficient. Since the war, and especially in the 1960s, the concentration of industry into large units was thought not only to be a natural feature of a mature economy, but also to embody economies of scale - in short, mergers and resulting concentration were thought of as an economic 'good'. The intense merger activity which followed has taken industrial concentration further in the UK than in any other industrialised nation. Of late, this fact has given rise to a re-examination of both the economic desirability of particular types of merger, and the wider effects of a very concentrated economy. Economies of scale have certainly been achieved through mergers in manufacturing, retail and distribution. However, the phrase 'diseconomies of scale' has been coined largely to describe the problems of unwieldly mergers. These have often been responsible for the deterioration in the performance of previously successful small units once they have been taken over. It is interesting that a current fashion is de-merging - in which small peripheral units are hived off from large conglomerates to go it alone as small units - perhaps via a management buyout.

Turning to longer term economic benefits, small firms are often claimed to be a source of innovation and dynamism in the economy. Can this claim be justified? Small firms do not have the resources to fund the scale of R&D necessary to produce innovations in, for example, aerospace, pharmaceuticals and motor vehicles. However, a study undertaken for the Bolton Committee of Inquiry on Small Firms(3) concluded that small firms made 'a large contribution' to industrial innovation in machinery, instruments and electronics. It also indicated that the growth of professional R&D in the large corporations has apparently not eliminated the contribution of small firms to industrial invention and innovation, and that the efficienty of innovation of small firms is greater than in the larger competitors. Problems arise for small firms in the high cost of patent fees, and particularly in the difficulty of funding the R&D work required <u>before</u> a project is in a sufficient stage of development to attract risk capital.

On the other hand, small firms may enjoy lower overhead costs, better communication and stronger motivation. The informality and flexibility of small firm structure lends itself to the cultivation and ripening of new ideas. Indeed, some large companies have gone so far as to try to simulate a small firm environment for those employees working on new product development.

In short, small firms are a source of dynamism and innovation in certain sectors of the economy where they have a chance to compete. Given the right conditions, they could contribute a great deal more.

WHAT CAN A LARGE FIRM DO?

If it is accepted that the encouragement of small firms will benefit the economy, how, then, can large firms contribute to this? Drawing on the experiences of large firms already working in this field, and on those of the London Enterprise Agency (LEntA) since it was set up in April 1979, 'what large firms can do' appears to split into two areas. The first is concerned with making the normal activities of large firms more helpful to small firms. This means framing personnel, commercial and corporate strategy policies which will help small firms (while not damaging their own interests). The second involves policies and expenditure outside the commercial sphere and nearer to the social responsibility programmes already pursued by many major companies.

i. 'Internal' Initiatives

When a company makes many people redundant, there will be a few (probably a handful) who will be willing and able to become self-employed. Some companies, notably ICI, have been very active in seeking out and supporting these people by laying on 'Start Your Own Business' training themselves, or by paying for employees to join similar courses elsewhere. In some cases, firms have provided start-up finance, or promised orders or service contracts in advance for fledgling businesses set up by ex-employees. An ICI executive involved in these programmes gave the following opinion at a conference organised by LEntA on the topic of large firms and small firms in February 1980:

> "Clearly there are significant numbers of people in ICI and, no doubt, in other companies, who have ideas in varying degrees of development about 'doing their own thing'. If economic pressures are to reduce jobs, and if these are matched by financial incentives and practical measures of help, then appreciable members of these people can be persuaded to move towards self-employment and the setting up of small businesses ... Without the particular sticks and carrots situation described. However, relatively few lower and middle management people seem prepared actually to give up their usually secure and pensionable jobs for the certain risks and uncertain gains of running their own businesses."

It is perhaps unfortunate that just those employees likely to make successsful businesses of their own - by and large the more entrepreneurial senior and middle managers and skilled craftsmen and technicians - are also those employees the large firms will be keen to retain. Firms, therefore, need to decide on their priorities if they are to avoid unwelcome consequences of a voluntary redundancy policy.

It is in the area of commercial policy - purchasing and supply - that large firms have their most obvious interface with small firms. It is also an area in which they have received much citicism, connected mainly with the slow payment of bills, and the exaction of onerous credit terms from small suppliers. While there must be scope for large companies to improve things in this department, there is growing interest in possibilities for an all-round improvement in the commercial relationships of small and large firms leading to greater efficiency in purchasing and supply for both sides.

The contention that markets do not work fruitfully for the purchasing and supply relations of small and large firms, largely to the detriment of small suppliers, has led to a number of projects around the country to investigate the problem. Some of these have been conceived with the simple aim of encouraging large firms to source more from local suppliers, a dubious idea from an efficiency point of view, and one likely to be met with scepticism by purchasing offices. These exist, after all, to find the most economic sources of supply for the company. If discrimination in favour of small local suppliers is adopted as company policy, instructions from a most senior level to the purchasing office would seem to be a requirement for the policy to have any effect.

But the various examinations of the problems of small firm suppliers and sub-contractors in the work done for the Birmingham Inner City Project, and the continuing work of the Welsh and Scottish Development Agencies, reveal a basis for action justifiable on sounder economic grounds. They show that the existence of an independent middleman - an engineer- working with both the buying department of a large firm and in close contact with local suppliers can effect increased business between large firms buying engineering supplies and sub-contract services, and small firms. The role of the independent middleman is to find out from large firms what commodities they have supply problems with - whether because of quality or availability or price - and communicate these opportunities to the small firms with whom they have spent time discovering their precise expertise and capacity.

Why is this function required? On the one side it is lack of marketing skills on the part of small sub-contractors and suppliers, who have traditionally been totally passive in their approach to getting business. On the other side, buyers do not necessarily have the time to research the skills and capacity of potential local suppliers, especially where new components are required and, therefore, become increasingly susceptible to the more sophisticated marketing methods of larger firms, including foreign suppliers.

The middleman can learn of current and future sub-contract opportunities by talking to large purchasing departments, and communicate these opportunities to small firms - in effect, act as the marketing department of the small firm. The long-term aim of this work must be to make small suppliers more aware of opportunities that exist and to help them develop the marketing skills necessary to exploit them. That needs cooperation from large firm buyers as well as organisational input from a third party.

A third area for 'internal initiatives' is the encouragement of 'management buyouts', in which managers and/or other investors buy out all or part of a company from the parent and run it as a separate business. In America, management buyouts are commonplace and have been for at least 15 years - ever since the first post war doubts were raised about the infallibility of bigness in business. It is a form of entrepreneurial activity relatively new in Britain, but one that seems to be growing.

Reasons for buyouts vary; they include large firms disposing of peripheral business activities acquired as by-products of mergers; enforced sale of assets to raise cash where the only buyers to come forward may be the existing managers; firms in receivership where the receiver may feel disposed towards selling to previous managers as opposed to rival bidders where other things are equal, and reaction against the trend of the 1960s which led companies to pull all services such as exhibition organisation, printing, etc in-house.

In the current economic climate, where large firms are all looking to prune expenditure, or may need to raise cash quickly, or are going into receivership, management buyouts may offer an efficient alternative to the waste of redundancy. Healthy sections of ailing giants can be salvaged as independent companies with good prospects.

A particularly good illustration of this is the story of the buyout by its managing director of Atcost, the Kent based fabricator of concrete and steel buildings. This company was bought up by the Lyon Construction Group in the mid-1970s, and 18 months later found itself being dragged into receivership with Lyon. Although a healthy company itself, Atcost had been loaded with debt and starved of cash by Lyon. It took 18 months for its directors to arrange a £600,000 institutional loan and equity package to add to their own £100,000 stake but, having bought it, after two-and-a-half years, their pre-tax profit grew 54% in 1980-81 while its debt/equity ratio fell from 14:1 to near parity.

ICFC, the financial institution with the heaviest commitment to buyouts (£15m in 1980-81), and the most experienced in handling them, has found them a safer investment than new companies. Whereas its failure rate with new enterprises is about one in three, ICFC knows of only seven failed management buyouts out of about 200 in recent years. This is understandable: in contrast to managers starting new business, the management of buyouts have knowledge of their business and an established basis from which to tackle all the problems associated with running their own business.

The large firm has a definite role to play in this process. A study of management buyouts by the Business Graduates Association (BGA)(4) recommends that 'large firm corporate plans should cover the eventuality that employees may wish to develop redundant units for themselves'. Where corporate planning leads to redundancy in plant and people, the firm may benefit from 'a conscious policy to minimise (the) adverse impacts on other people by ensuring continuity of employment and business resources. The employees may be the best people to ensure this continuity in certain circumstances'. It continues by pointing out that survey findings show production companies as the most reluctant to spin-off units and yet could benefit from consistency in their operations by dropping obsolescent or unrelated production facilities and products at the appropriate time. They might consider the possibility that their staff would be willing to run their own units if cash could be raised ...'

The report also raises the point that with regard to long-term profitability of their company, the immediate interests of employees and wider responsibilities to people and organisations within their localities, should influence vendor directors away from securing the best possible price where management buyout teams are concerned in the bidding. The price a management team has to pay to its parent-vendor can have a significant effect on the future success or failure of the venture.

At the opposite end of the large firm's corporate policy spectrum is the question of investment of risk capital in new ventures. While there is no question that firms participating in new venture capital funds are looking to make good profits, they have made a contribution to innovation through financing small firms with high risk ideas. There is evidence that small firms, particularly with ideas in areas of high technology, find it difficult to raise capital from traditional sources. Part of the reason has been identified as lack of expertise by city institutions in assessing risk connected with high technology ventures. The Prudential Assurance Company have grasped this problem by setting up Prutec, an investment subsidiary, which will be managed by Patcentre International, a consultancy with acknowledged expertise in the assessment and appraisal of technological projects.

Similarly, Rainford Venture Capital, a subsidiary of Pilkington Brothers, also backed by BP, Prudential Assurance and ICFC, and set up in February 1980, has hired Venture Founders Limited to appraise applicants for funds. Venture Founders has been involved in launching rapid growth companies in Canada and the US over the last 10 years, and therefore has some experience in assessing likely projects.

An alternative to the simple provision of funds is for a large company to take on involvement in developing a product or invention conceived outside the company, but where the inventor has no means to cover the development of a product to a stage where it begins to pay for itself.

The LEntA has had experience in handling new products and innovations which could not be properly exploited without the development resources at the disposal of a large firm. This experience has made it clear that the prospect of a mutually advantageous arrangement being made between an inventor and an established large firm can be increased enormously by an independent third party being involved to sort out the inevitable misunderstandings that are likely along the route to a mutually beneficial agreement.

ii. 'External' Activities

Outside their normal activities, the scope for large firms to help small is extremely wide, because of the many resources at their disposal which can be made available to small firms at really very little cost.

In most cases, large firms find these resources more effectively used as part of a consortium. The consortium may be a number of firms based on a Chamber of Commerce, as are LEntA, Leeds Business Venture, The Birmingham Venture, Aid to Bristol Enterprises, or with local authorities, eg. Business Link at Runcorn, or a local college, as in the close cooperation between ICI and Teesside Polytechnic.

Whatever grouping the large firm joins to help small firms, close cooperation with the local authorities, existing business organisations and local educational establishments will widen the scope of the operation, and allow resources made available more efficient use. These resources can include personnel, finance for research, sponsorship and premises.

a. Personnel

There are at least three different ways in which personnel from large firms can be deployed to help small firms. The first is where a company is prepared to make a manager available outside his firm on a term secondment of one to two years, to work in an enterprise agency or local business advice service. The secondee might be expected to take up counselling work related to his own professional specialisation, eg. marketing or finance, or to act as a project organiser.

Executive secondments are a fairly new departure, and lessons are still being learned about what makes for a successful secondment, both for the secondee in his future career development, and for the organisation to which he is seconded.

What is clear is that the more independent and extrovert secondee is likely to adapt more readily to the office environment and lack of large firm support services found in the typical secondment posting.

Capacity to adapt to the frequently unsophisticated enquiries from small firm clients is a vital requirement.

Shorter term secondments of up to three months can provide valuable project work for offices helping small firms allowing research, feasibility studies and accounts to be done at far lower cost than using outside consultants.

A third use of large company personnel is as consultants and experts for one-off enquiries in which technical or specialist skills are required by small firms. Expert help in areas like computer use, factory layout, or new product design can therefore be provided at low cost. The availability of large firm experts is undoubtedly of great value but, certainly in the experience of LEntA, it requires careful handling if it is to work. The large firm 'expert' cannot be expected to do more than give 'one-off' advice. Our experience is that small firms often do not follow up advice given, or fail to press for further help if an initial consultation is not enough. It is therefore essential for such consultations to be arranged, attended and followed up by a third party, probably an adviser who has a longer term relationship with the small firm. Where the 'expert' and the small firm are simply put in touch, it is highly unlikely that a satisfactory outcome will ensue. If large firms make members of their staff available as experts to help small firms, it should be recognised that a great deal of effort has to go into making these arrangements work, and that successful outcomes depend very largely upon the personality and commitment of the executives involved.

b. Finance

Not all large firms that wish to help small firms want the level of involvement that secondments and participation in enterprise agencies and trusts entail. However, there is plenty of scope for use of funds in both research and small firm promotion. High quality research into small firms' problems is a prerequisite of any effective lobbying of government. Where the government shares a particular concern as, for example, in the case of the shortage of small workshop and factory units cited below, high quality research can be funded by the taxpayer. On more contentious issues it is important that funds are available for independent research. This should, on the face of it, carry far more weight with governments than, for example, a survey of members of a small firms' pressure group (although exceptions here are cited in Ava Westrip's paper on changes in employment legislation elsewhere in this volume).

Apart from research for political lobbying, funds are required for feasibility studies on the various schemes suggested to help small firms. In 1980, LEntA produced a feasibility study on provision of central services for small firm industrial estates, and another on additional market opportunities for London's traditional industries. Both of these have been important tools in decision-making about allocation of available resources to various possible initiatives.

Funds can also find effective use in the organisation of exhibitions to promote small firms' products, or to subsidise stands at trade fairs. Trade fairs represent enormous expenditure relative to the budget of small firms, and consequently participation involves high risk. On the other hand, they offer a vital form of exposure to trade buyers. In 1980, LEntA subsidised a private exhibition for small firms in London to meet buyers from major department stores, following events held by COSIRA and the Scottish Council. Many of the firms taking part would not normally have had the opportunity to meet these buyers.

LEntA has also sponsored businesses and individuals with newly-developed products and ideas to take part in exhibitions such as the Sunday Times 'Business to Business' exhibition, where they could meet the investors and partners necessary to take these ideas forward. It is important to be able to offer this opportunity free of charge because, with products in early stages of development, availability of funds for taking part in an exhibition is likely to be nil.

Finally, funds can usefully be made available to sponsor business competitions. This is a form of sponsorship which has obvious publicity pay-offs for a large firm. The benefits to the small firm can be considerable, too: if it wins, cash, other tangible rewards and some useful publicity are forthcoming and, even if it does not win, the discipline of articulating a business plan is often highly useful. Typical was a competition run jointly by Mobil and the Design Council in early 1981 offered competitors the chance to win £10,000, free marketing advice and exposure in an exhibition for the top 50 entrants paid for by the organisers.

c. Premises

Finally, there is the question of premises. Various researchers have pointed out the extreme importance of availability of suitable premises to the birth and expansion of new businesses. The shortage of small units, and particularly the very small units required for start-ups (500-1500 sq ft), was confirmed in a Coopers and Lybrand report for the Department of Industry published in 1980(5). As a result, the 1980 Budget introduced tax incentives for the building of new small units above 2000 sq ft, particularly in the provinces, in areas where sites are readily available. However, very small units, particularly in urban areas, remain in short supply.

This is an area in which large firms can play a role, notably where they find themselves with redundant inner city sites and factories that could be adapted to provide small firm premises. Redundant sites, such as the one in Wandsworth made available to LEntA by Shell UK, can be used for purpose-built small units, while old factories can be divided up and converted for the same purpose. It will often be impossible to do this work on a commercial basis, leaving rentals low enough to be attractive to small firms, nor are all old factories suitable for conversion inexpensively (although factory conversions are potentially the greatest source of small units in the future).

Despite these problems, many large companies are active in the provision of premises and interest is growing in this means of re-investment in buildings made redundant by plant closure. BSC, Unilever and Pilkingtons, for example, provide start-up units as part and parcel of their small firm activities. Meanwhile, LEntA Properties has recently been formed by some of LEntA's member companies to provide inner city units. Their first project will be the conversion of a derelict multi-storey grain house in London's East End.

CONCLUSION

It is now nearly three years since Pocock, speaking in the Ashridge Lecture(6) on behalf of large firms, said: "If we believe that small companies are a necessary part of the economy, we must pay more than lip service".

It is worth recalling the suggestions he made then of what big companies might do in pursuit of these ends. Briefly, he said they might:

i. resist the temptation to use bargaining power to a point that stretches the resources of the small business unfairly;

ii. establish a management policy recognising the value of small enterprise, and support this in action;

iii. pursue a more enlightened purchasing and contract policy recognising the limits of order size and contract value the small man can stand;

iv. help small local firms with site, space and equipment surplus to the large firm's needs;

v. join with other firms to provide advice on opportunities for small business growth;

vi. provide financial pump priming for small firms when setting up;

vii. offer specialist help to small firms, eg. with accounting;

viii. help innovators in the early stages of product development.

Pocock's proposals are a useful set of criteria by which to judge the progress made so far. On some of the points there is undoubted momentum. The provision of help, either through enterprise agencies or through internal company programmes has developed dramatically. There are now agencies or trusts in London, Birmingham, Bristol, Leeds, St Helens, Halton, Hackney, the Wirral and Walsall, with others in formation in Leicester, Manchester, Cornwall and a number of other centres. The interest in such ventures is moving forward, although there is a danger that the push is coming from central and local government, which rather negates the established view that agencies and trusts work best when the initiative comes from a committed private sector. Some local ventures could face difficulties by being pushed too far, too soon.

In connection with the help given to agencies and trusts, large firms have concentrated on providing help with premises, including conversion and new buildings, plus offering specialist help in areas such as accounting and innovation. There has also been help for training programmes and some firms have started in-house programmes to help employees start their own businesses.

However, both for the agencies and the individual major firms, it will be the next steps that will be important. The agencies will have to decide whether they remain as passive counselling operations or whether they wish to become more deeply embedded in their communities and to become agents for change. In particular, the agencies have to consider developing their role as catalysts in helping firms to grow. This involves not only pinpointing prospects with potential, but marshalling the resources to facilitate their growth.

In the longer term, the relationship between the agencies and Chambers of Commerce will have to be determined. In some ways the development of the agency movement is a commentary on the reluctance of the Chambers of Commerce to play an active as opposed to a passive role in their communities. Either through the support of large firms or local authorities, or both, the agencies can harness resources which hitherto have been denied to the Chambers; in the long run their objectives are complementary.

The most notable lack of progress by Pocock's set of criteria has been in the operation of large companies' commercial policy. In a way this is not surprising, in that for many companies support given to agencies and trusts has already represented a radical change of policy. It is also being rather ambitious to expect much progress in an area like purchasing in the middle of a deep recession. There are some hopeful signs but the testing time will come when the economy picks up and large firms start to look for suppliers. Will they plan ahead to find small firms in the UK, or will they leave it to the last minute and look abroad?

However, the most important aspect of large firms' involvement on the small firms 'bandwagon' is that they can play a part, if not the major role, in ensuring that it moves from a rather woolly concept tinged with a romantic hue to a fundamental switch of resources into a determined effort to achieve real growth.

REFERENCES

1. Pocock, C C, More Jobs: A small cure for a big problem, The Ashridge Lectue, 1977.

2. Birch, D L, The Job Generation Process, MIT Program on Neighborhood and Regional Change, Cambridge, Mass, 1979.

3. Freeman, C, The Role of Small Firms in Innovation in the UK since 1945, Research Report No 6, Committee of Inquiry on Small Firms, HMSO, London, 1971.

4. Stanway, R, The Successful Spin-Off, Business Graduates Association, London, 1980.

5. Provision of Small Industrial Premises, Coopers and Lybrand Associates Ltd for the Department of Industry, London, 1980.

6. Pocock, C, op cit.

5 Local authority assistance to small firms

PETER WILSON
London Business School

BACKGROUND

Over the last few years, local authorities have developed an increasingly interventionist approach to the encouragement of small business (particularly new business) on the basis that herein lie the greatest new job gains. While this policy is generally not in dispute, there is some confusion about the criteria used by local authorities for the selection of small business for assistance. Although most local authorities claim that their overriding objective is the maximisation of employment opportunities, their assistance tends not to be job orientated, but rather problem orientated. Besides this inherent conflict, there are additional inconsistencies because most local authorities simply do not know what the real problems of local small firms are, preferring to place their subsidy where their traditional responsibilities and the perceived needs of small firms overlap.

This article briefly describes two research studies: the first investigated local authority policies and practices towards small business and the second looked more closely at one particular interface between small business and the local authority. The latter study investigated the characteristics, problems and job creation potential of small business in an inner London borough to establish criteria for the selection of firms for assistance by the local authorty.

THE SURVEY OF LOCAL AUTHORITIES

The rationale for intervention by local authorities to promote small business is based on four premises. First, local authorities are, by definition, local, and are therefore close to small firms; second, their statutory duties oblige them to intervene in the local economy anyway; third, relatively small quantities of subsidy can create substantial benefits for the local community; and fourth, most small firms depend on the local market rather than on distant markets. The scope for local authority intervention to assist local firms is therefore potentially considerable, and a growing number of authorities are actively encouraging firms to set up and expand in their areas.

To determine the nature and extent of intervention, in August 1979 the chief executives of 158 local authorities in England and Wales were sent a short questionnaire requesting details of their policies and practices towards small business. The responses are set out in Table 1.

Table 1: Local Authority Survey - Response Rates

Authority	Mailed	Responded	Response Rate (%)
County Councils	53	42	79.2
London Boroughs	34	24	70.6
District Councils	71	48	67.6
Total	158	114	72.2

Research Findings

1. A large number of local authorities (45) had no small business programme at all, nor did they give any recognition in their policies to the different needs of small and large firms. The remainder claimed to have either a specific small business programme (43) or an approach that differentiated to some extent between small and large firms (26).

2. The authorities with a specific small business programme provided a wide range of services, of which premises was the most popular element, as shown in Table 2. Information and counselling services ranked second and financial assistance ranked third. Trade promotion, housing and training were of little significance in local authority programmes. Those authorities with a non-specific but differentiated programme based their assistance on indirect measures such as the orientation of their employment policies to small business, the encouragement of small premises construction and assistance with finding small factory units.

Table 2: Actions under Specific Small Business Programmes

Actions	Responses f	%*
1. Providing small premises and workshops	42	97.7
2. Providing information; directory of services	17	39.5
3. Industrial liaison officer; counsellors	14	32.6
4. Grants	12	27.9
5. Loans and loan guarantees	12	27.9
6. Liaison with COSIRA, SFIC, ARC, etc	11	25.6
7. Provision for small business in structure plans	8	18.6
8. Providing sites for small business	5	11.6
9. Trade promotion	4	9.3
10. Key worker housing scheme	1	2.3
11. Employee training assistance	1	2.3

*of the 43 authorities with specific programmes

3. Only 44 authorities claimed to have criteria for selecting small firms for assistance. Table 3 shows that most criteria related to employment, although a few authorities were committed to encouraging small business on more general terms.

Table 3: Selection Criteria used by Local Authorities

Criteria	Responses f	%*
Creating new jobs, maximising employment	34	77.3
Viability	22	50.0
Creating new firms, new wealth, diversification	14	31.8
Saving jobs	6	13.6
Planning and environmental problems	6	13.6
Start-ups, smallest firms	5	11.4
Failure to get assistance elsewhere	4	9.1
Manufacturing industry	4	9.1
Exporters	1	2.3

*of the 44 authorities using criteria

4. The major problems of small firms as perceived by local authorities were usually discovered as the result of contact with local firms by council employees either in the day-to-day execution of their responsibilities in the local area or in their special commitments to small firms. Their perceptions were therefore very much subjective, reflecting the established contact areas between business and local authority. Several authorities (17) had undertaken research to identify the major problems of local firms, although none had extended the research to identify the firms providing the largest number of new jobs. Table 4 sets out the major problems perceived by local authorities in their normal contact with local firms and contrasts these with the problems identified empirically by the 17 authorities mentioned above.

Table 4: Ranking of the Perceived and Actual Problems of Small Firms

Problem	Ranking of Problems	
	Perceived by Authorities	Identified by Surveys
Lack of suitable premises	1	1
Lack of finance, access to finance	2	4
Shortage of labour	3	3
Administration, management	4	8
Inadequate parking, access, loading	5	2
Lack of information and assistance	6	6
Planning constraints	7	5
Inadequate public transport	8	7
Decline in market	9	9
High rates	10	10

Although in both the perceived and identified cases financial problems were found to be important, it is interesting that the surveys identified finance as a somewhat less important problem than the physical attributes of the building and the area, such as parking, access and loading. Another difference was the attitude to administration and bureaucracy which the surveys identified as being of little importance to the small business Both the declining market and high rates were considered to be of negligible importance in both cases, although this may have reflected the greater buoyancy in the economy at the time of the research.

Conclusions

The tendency of many local authorities to intervene in the local economy on the side of small business is confirmed by this survey, although many have so far eschewed deliberate policies to create jobs through small business. Indeed, in several cases local authorities were actively discouraging the growth of new enterprise on the groups that such policies would, over a period of time, necessitate large commitments to local infrastructure. Only seven of those authorities without a small business programme planned to introduce one in the near future.

The major impetus for local authority action came from the alleged shortage of small premises, although few authorities had objectively determined the nature and extent of the problems and needs of small firms. The emphasis on premises is overwhelming and reflects the tendency to intervene where assistance is most visible. It is clearly possible that a shortage of small premises exists in certain areas, but the extent of this problem in relation to other perceived problems appears to be overstated by local authorities. For instance, although the shortage of labour and various physical constraints (parking and access) were identified in the local authority surveys (Table 4) as being of major importance, there is little, if any, recognition of these in local authority actions (Table 2).

If there are substantial differences between the needs of small firms as perceived by local authorities and their real needs, it is likely that resources are being wasted on attempts to redress the perceived problems. Some of the solutions to the real problems lie more easily in the local authority domain. For instance, the provision of parking permits for small firms is easily implemented, while the provision of finance is not. Nor is the latter a traditional local authority responsibility, and it is therefore likely to be costly while the learning curve is climbed.

There is no evidence that local authorities can select firms for assistance on the basis of their job generating potential when faced with a larger number of 'eligible' firms than assistance resources can satisfy. This may not be a problem in the less prosperous parts of the country (where any employment is better than none at all), but where a limited amount of subsidy is available and the question becomes one of which firms to select, the general criterion of employment maximisation requires further refinement. For instance, should subsidy go to the smallest and newest firms or to established firms already employing over (say) 100 persons; should subsidy go to manufacturers or to service firms; should subsidy go to firms with unstable histories but with considerable potential for job creation? Local authorities cannot place their subsidy where the employment creating effects are greatest simply because they do not know which firms have the greatest job creating potential. Their actions therefore are orientated towards problem-solving, as problems are the most visible expression of the needs of small firms, even though they provide a second-best solution. Moreover, this survey has shown that the identification of real problems has not been undertaken systematically by local authorities; nor have they consistently implemented programmes which are designed to alleviate the identified problems, preferring to place their subsidy in the most visible problem areas.

THE SMALL BUSINESS SURVEY

The two major unanswered issues arising from the survey of local authorities related to how local authorities could best assist firms and which firms should be assisted. To explore these issues, a sample of small firms was selected for investigation and analysis in the London Borough of Camden, identified as a typical inner city area where small businesses were of some importance in providing jobs for local residents. The area was a mixture of old and new, rich and poor; the contiguousness of affluence in one part and deprivation in another was itself expected to provide market opportunities for small firms. But affluence and deprivation among the local populace were not the only exceptional demographic characteristics: the multiple paradoxes of opportunity and despair, labour shortages and unemployment and dynamic entrepreneurship and mere business survival were others.

The population of Camden in 1977 was under 200,000, and a large share of employment was in banking and services (35.9%) and distribution and hotels (20.8%), with a smaller minority in manufacturing (14.2%). The distribution of employment and number of firms by size of establishment is given in Table 5. The dependence of the area for employment on smaller firms (or at least, establishments) is clear from this table. Not only are most firms in the area very small (98.4% employ fewer than 200 persons each), but these firms account for a relatively greater share of employment in the Camden borough than in the country as a whole.

Table 5: Distribution of Establishments and Employment in the Borough and the Respondents by Size of Establishment

Area	Size of Establishment (No of Employees)					
	1-5 cum %	6-25 cum %	26-50 cum %	51-100 cum %	101-200 cum %	201+ cum %
Borough						
Establishments	54.6	86.3	92.9	96.6	98.4	100
Employees	6.5	24.3	35.4	47.8	59.9	100
Respondents						
Firms	34.7	82.8	88.6	95.4	99.2	100
Employees	4.5	30.0	38.9	57.1	100	-

Objectives and Methodology

The objectives were to identify the major problems and constraints facing small firms in the borough and to establish criteria for selecting firms for local authority assistance.

Small firms were identified, for the purposes of the study, as those which were independent (not part of larger firms), generally owner-managed or closely held and employing fewer than 250 persons. It was not possible to conform rigidly to the definition in all cases, simply because it was not always possible to determine the nature of the firm before the interview. Any deviations were not likely to influence the results significantly.

The sample of small firms was drawn from two sources and included only manufacturing, construction, wholesale distribution and certain services; retailing, financial services and most professional services, such as accountants and solicitors, were excluded. The main sample was randomly drawn from Kellys London Street Directory 1979, consisting of 200 firms which were thought to conform to the above general definition. On careful investigation it was found that 11 of them fell outside the definition, leaving a usable sample of 189 small firms. The sample was drawn from two areas of the borough where small firms were concentrated. Because very new firms were under-represented in this sample (the compilation of the Directory explains this), an additional sample of 19 firms recently established in the area was drawn from the rates list, representing mainly new businesses under 5 years old.

The firms in the sample were contacted first by letter, then by telephone to arrange an interview. From the usable sample of small firms, the following response rates emerged.

Table 6: Response Rates of Small Business Survey

	Random Sample	Rates List Sample	Total
usable firms	189	19	208
responses	85	19	104
response rate (%)	45	100	50

The reasons for non-response can be attributed either to the non-availability of the proprietor or manager, or to the inability to make contact with the business at all. In the case of the former, the usual response was either 'no time', or 'not interested'. In a few cases the relevant person could not be contacted. In the case of the latter, either the business had moved away (this could be confirmed in a few instances) or it had ceased to function. This was generally assumed to

Table 7: The Distribution of Small Firms: The Respondents, the Sample and the Camden Universe

SIC*	Respondents 104 firms		Total Sample 208 firms	Camden** 9931 firms
	No	%	%	%
2. Minerals, manufacture of metals, chemicals, other	-	-	2.4	0.9
3. Metal goods, engineering & vehicles industry	16	15.4	14.9	4.4
4. Other manufacturing	38	36.5	32.2	8.8
5. Construction	7	6.7	8.2	3.9
6. Distribution, hotels, catering, repairs	27	26.0	26.0	42.0
7. Transport & communications	2	1.9	1.4	4.1
8. Banking, finance, insurance	12	11.5	13.5	30.6
9. Other services	2	1.9	1.4	5.2
Total	104	100	100	100

*the SIC referred to in the text is the 1980 revision

**employing fewer than 200 persons

be the case when no telephone number was available, the letter was returned unopened or the premises looked deserted when visited by the interviewer. In a few instances, cessation was confirmed by a search at Companies House.

To complete the financial profile of small firms in the sample, a search was undertaken at Companies House to determine the turnover and pre-tax profits of the registered companies for the financial year 1975-76 to 1977-78. The results of the surveys and the Companies House data were computerised.

The total sample of 208 small firms represented 2.06% of all establishments in the borough. A breakdown of the respondent firms by SIC, together with the distribution of firms in the universe (the borough) is provided in Table 7.

RESULTS OF THE SURVEY

General

Most firms were independent limited companies (62.5%); there were only eight subsidiaries (7.7%). The remainder were partnerships and sole proprietorships. Thus decision-making in nearly every case lay with the owner-manager or professional manager in the small independent business. In addition, the premises visited were invariably the sole office of the business or the head office (89.4%). The average age of the businesses interviewed was 27 years, the youngest being under one year old and the oldest 140 years.

Table 8: Age of the Business

Years	Responses	
	f	%
0-5	23	22.1
6-10	14	13.5
11-25	28	26.9
26-50	24	23.1
51-100	12	11.6
over 100	3	2.9
Total	104	100

Employment

The average employment per firm was 23 persons, of which 15 were males and eight females. Total employment in the 104 firms interviewed was 2408 persons, representing 1.1% of the total employed labour force in the borough. The smallest firms employed one person and the largest 400 persons. Most firms were very small, with over one third employing up to five persons and nearly 90% employing less than 50 persons. The comparative data for all firms in the borough are given in Table 5. With the exception of the smallest firms (fewer than six persons), the sample conforms fairly closely to the distribution of total employment. The reason for under-representation at the lowest level is explained by the absence of sufficient new or very young firms from the sample, an unavoidable shortcoming caused by the nature of the sample source.

The average small firm employed the majority of its workforce from outside the borough, although very few from outside Greater London. On average, some 32% of employees lived locally in the borough, 63% in the rest of Greater London and only 5% lived outside London.

A large proportion of firms (24%) actually employed no local people, while only a very small proportion (12.5%) drew over 80% of their workforce from the local area. Only 16.3% employed any labour at all from outside Greater London.

Of the 48 firms reporting a net change in their total workforce over the past year, 126 jobs were created and 108 jobs were lost, representing a net gain of 18 jobs. There was an average net change of five jobs per firm in either direction. About one half of all firms experienced no change in their workforce.

Table 9: Net Change in Workforce: Past Year and Next Year

	Past Year		Next Year	
Change in Jobs	f	%	f	%
+ 11-20	1	1.0	2	2.0
+ 6-10	7	7.1	7	7.1
+ 1-5	18	18.4	28	28.3
no change	50	51.0	59	59.6
- 1-5	16	16.3	3	3.0
- 6-10	5	5.1	-	-
- 11-20	1	1.0	-	-
Total	98*	100	99*	100

*a few respondents would not reveal changes

Over the next year a rather different pattern emerges. Most firms (59.6%) anticipated no change, while only 3% anticipated a net decrease in their workforce. A large number of firms (37.4%) was quite optimistic about creating jobs in the next year. Of the 40 firms anticipating a change in their workforce, 154 jobs were expected to be created for the loss of only nine jobs, a net gain of 145 jobs.

These findings should be interpreted cautiously, particularly as the past year had produced so few net new jobs, and these in a marginally more buoyant economic climate. The surprising optimism of the responses may reflect the independence of the local economy from the world at large, the atypical nature of local activities or the necessarily poor planning abilities of businessmen in the small firms.

In order to substantiate the realism of the above forecasts of employment generation over the next year, firms were then asked about the number and type of existing vacancies. The total number of vacancies recorded was 156, which is roughly equivalent to the 154 jobs expected to be created over the next year. This was an average of one-and-a-half jobs per firm. Most vacancies were in the skilled (39.1%) and semi-skilled (33.3%) categories.

Finance and Financial Aspects

Financial data collected in the interviews were supplemented by searching company records at Companies House. The results are incomplete, however, and should be interpreted cautiously.

Table 10: Average Turnover, Profits and Losses, 1975 to 1979

Year	Average Turnover (£000)	Average Profits (£000)	Recorded Losses (Frequency)
1975-76	1963	79	7
1976-77	2028	81	15
1977-78	2529	99	5
1978-79	1656	81	11

The much lower averages for the 1978-79 financial year reflect the water different composition of the respondents, who included the smaller firms which did not usually submit returns to Companies House. The smallness of the typical firm is further illustrated by the very low modal turnover range of under £100,000 and a median turnover of £181,230 in the financial year 1978-79.

Table 11: Annual Turnover and Profits 1978-79

Turnover (£)			Profits (£)		
Category	f	%	Category	f	%
0-100,000	37	42.0	Loss	11	17.2
100,001-500,000	24	27.3	1-25,000	38	59.4
500-001-1m	10	11.4	25,001-100,000	6	9.4
1m-5m	12	13.6	100,001-200,000	4	6.3
over 5m	5	5.7	over 200,000	5	7.8
Total	88*	100		64*	100

*a few respondents would not reveal financial data

Finally, some idea of the profitability of the respondent firms is provided below (the ratio is pre-tax profits to turnover, providing a net profit ratio).

Table 12: Net Profit Ratios 1975-1978

Net Profit	1975-76		1976-77		1977-78	
%	f	%	f	%	f	%
0-5	13	59.1	15	65.2	16	69.6
6-10	3	13.6	3	13.0	2	8.7
11-15	3	13.6	2	8.7	2	8.7
16-20	1	4.5	1	4.3	1	4.3
over 20	2	9.1	2	8.6	2	8.6
Total	22*	100	23*	100	23*	100

*most firms were not in a position to provide detailed data

The rather few recordings above provide too small a basis for analysis. The only observation worth making is that relatively few firms appeared to be in a very profitable position, although this conclusion would have to be seen in the light of trends for the relevant industry before judgement could be passed.

Premises

One half of firms occupied premises with an area of less than 2000 sq ft, while only 14% were in premises over 10,000 sq ft. The average size of premises was 6570 sq ft, although the median size was only 2061 sq ft. Most firms (77.9%) leased or rented their premises (the remainder owned them), paying an average rental of £1.75 per square foot. The median rental was £1.52 per square foot. Only 11.4% of firms paid over £2.50 per square foot.

Location

Nearly two thirds of firms (65.4%) had been in their present position less than 10 years, while only three firms had remained in their same premises for more than 50 years. A surprisingly small proportion (26.9%) had never relocated since inception, while most (43.3%) had relocated from within the borough and 24% from elsewhere in Greater London.

A Ranking of Major Problems

The problems of the respondents were recorded under each of the above headings, together with problems in the marketplace, with suppliers, training, the local authority and the physical environment. At the end of the survey the respondents were asked to rank the problems facing them at the time.

Table 13: Ranked Problems

Description	Most Important Problem		Second Important Problem		Third Important Problem		All Problems Identified	
	f	%	f	%	f	%	f	%*
Labour shortage	19	18.3	11	18.0	2	9.1	32	32
Economic downturn	17	16.3	5	8.2	7	31.8	29	29
Premises	12	11.5	3	4.9	-	-	15	15
Rates and Rentals	11	10.6	5	8.2	1	4.5	17	17
Internal problems	9	8.7	6	9.8	3	13.6	18	18
Cashflow	6	5.8	6	9.8	4	18.2	16	16
Unreliable supplies	5	4.8	4	6.6	1	4.5	10	10
Deteriorating environment	5	4.8	2	3.3	-	-	7	7
Other	16	15.4	19	31.1	4	18.2	39	39
(None)	(4)	(3.8)	-	-	-	-	-	-
Total	104	100	61	100	22	100	183	100

*of 100 firms reporting problems

The shortage of labour was the major concern of the firms in the sample, followed closely by market-related problems. These two problems were also the most frequently mentioned of all problems, accounting for one third of all problems identified. Although premises ranked as the third most important problem, of all problems mentioned it only ranked sixth, reflecting the greater concern with internal matters and the management of the business.

Table 14: Major Problems by Size of Firm

Major Problems	Size of Firm (No of Employees)		
	1-25 Firms %	Over 25 Firms %	Total Firms %
1. Labour shortage	84.4	15.6	100
2. Economic recession	75.7	24.3	100
3. Internal issues	66.7	33.3	100
4. Rates and rentals	88.2	11.8	100
5. Debtors and cashflow	81.3	18.7	100
6. Premises	100.0	-	100
7. Supplier unreliability	90.0	10.0	100
8. Deteriorating environment	57.1	42.9	100
9. Other	89.7	10.3	100
Total	82.0	18.0	100
Total problems	152	31	183
Percentage	83.1	16.9	100

The smallest firms ranked their major problems rather differently from the larger ones, putting premises and rates and rentals joint third in the table. It is also remarkable that no firms employing more than 25 persons were concerned about premises. If the smallest (and, by implication, newest) firms were experiencing greater problems than their larger neighbours, there is some support for the inference that start-ups and embryonic ventures will face the same constraints in the local economy. Neither of these two very important groups of small firms was represented in the survey (they are hard to identify, particularly on a random basis) although, as we have seen, the selection of a small number of firms recently established in the borough was an attempt to remedy this imbalance.

The ranking of these major problems differs substantially from the major problems perceived by local authorities (Table 4) and their action programmes (Table 2). Problems with premises were not as important as Table 2 suggests, although for the smallest firms in the sample this does appear to be the case. When locational differences are taken into account, the attention devoted by local authorities to premises appears to be inconsistent with the major problems of small firms. Interestingly, finance did not rank as a major problem in the survey, although local authorities in general gave this considerable prominence. On the other hand, problems in the market and high rates were considered to be important to the firms, yet they were not perceived by local authorities as being important, ranking at the bottom of the 'batting order' in Table 4.

One explanation for this apparent mismatch of real and perceived problems is that local authorities find it easier to act in certain areas and not in others, and will therefore take the line of least resistance, particularly if this lies in the direction of their normal responsibilities. But in the case of market problems, for example, the leverage available by using the substantial procurement needs of the authorities themselves is sufficient to create local jobs (or save them) in a more cost-effective and less risky way than providing finance for small firms. Large companies could also be persuaded to purchase locally where economies were available or buyers were not aware of the products and services produced in the local economy (or even where inertia prevented an efficient market developing), and it is surprising to see how few local authorities are resorting to trade promotion as a part of their small business programmes. With the possibility of tighter budgets in the future, local authorities will need to examine their small business activities and to decide where the greatest benefit can be obtained from a given quantum of subsidy. There is some evidence that they are not meeting the real needs of small firms and that considerable wastage of resources may be taking place.

CRITERIA FOR SELECTING FIRMS FOR ASSISTANCE

Having established what the problems of local small firms were, the research focussed on which firms might be selected for assistance.

The fundamental criterion for council assistance is the generation of the maximum number of jobs in the longer term (Table 3). In sympathy with this criterion the responses in the small business survey were analysed to show which firms were likely to create the most jobs. In the absence of data recording the actual changes in employment in the individual firm over a period of time (between five and ten years), a number of surrogates were used:

a. change in the workforce in the previous year

b. number of vacancies at present

c. percentage of local residents employed

These three employment generating 'indicators' were cross-tabulated with the size of the firm (number of employees or annual turnover), the age of the firm and financial performance. In addition, on the basis that jobs are likely to be maximised by firms with strong local linkages, the analysis included the relationships between firms and the location of their customers and suppliers.

a. Change in the Workforce in the Previous Year

Size of the Firm

The creation of net new jobs (job gains less job losses) was recorded for each employment size band.

Table 15: Size of Firm by Changes in Employment Last Year

	Employment Changes						
	Losses		No Change	Gains		Total	
Size of Firm (employees)	Firms (%)	Jobs	Firms (%)	Firms (%)	Jobs	Firms (%)	Jobs
1-25	71.4	47	92.8	69.2	57	82.5	10
26-50	9.5	14	3.6	7.7	20	5.8	6
51-100	9.5	8	3.6	11.5	19	6.8	11
Over 100	9.5	9	-	11.5	27	4.9	18
Total	100	78	100	100	123	100	45

Proportionately more of the smaller firms (employing fewer than 26 persons) did not experience a change in employment over the past year. Proportionately fewer small firms both lost jobs and gained them, while the opposite was true of firms employing more than 25 persons. The smaller firms also lost more jobs (47) than the larger firms (31) while gaining fewer (57) than the larger firms (66). In addition, the larger firms generated substantially more net new jobs over the past year. The smaller firms accounted for only 22.2% of all net new jobs while their contribution to total employment in the borough was 40.5%, and the largest firms (over 100 employees) accounted for 40% of net new jobs while contributing only 20.1% of employment in the borough (the contribution of the large firms employing over 200 persons is not taken into account in these comparisons). Therefore, the firms which seemed to create the most net new jobs were not the smallest, as is usually supposed, but those in the size band 101-200 employees.

Performance

The findings in relation to pre-tax profits 1978-79 are produced in Table 16. They show conclusively that in both absolute and relative terms the firms with the greatest profits (over £25,000 per annum) created the most net new jobs.

Table 16: Turnover and Profit in 1978-79 by Changes in the Workforce Last Year

	Changes in Employment						
	Losses		No Change	Gains		Total	
Category	Firms (%)	Jobs	Firms (%)	Firms (%)	Jobs	Firms (%)	Jobs
Turnover							
Up to £1m	70.0	44	91.1	68.2	73	80.5	29
Over £1m	30.0	32	8.9	31.8	40	19.5	8
Total	100	76	100	100	113	100	37
Profit/Loss							
Loss	37.5	25	6.9	15.8	28	17.2	3
Up to £25000	43.8	18	79.3	42.1	33	59.4	15
Over £25000	18.7	16	13.8	42.1	40	23.4	24
Total	100	59	100	100	101	100	42

The relationships between changes in turnover and profits are presented in Table 17, although the findings should be treated with due caution because of the incompleteness of the raw data. In terms of annual turnover between 1975 and 1978, the firms creating the most net new jobs were those with unstable histories (turnover increasing and decreasing) and those with increases over the period. The incomplete data make any conclusions tentative, but the main finding is that firms with unstable histories did create a relatively large number of net new jobs In terms of changes in profits between 1975-78, again the findings show that unstable firms did create a large number of net new jobs.

Table 17: Job Creation and Performance of the Firm

Performance Variable	Net Job Changes	
	Firms %	Jobs
Turnover Change 1975-78		
2 year decline	7.7	- 7
1 year decline, 1 year increase	15.4	+ 9
2 year increase	76.9	+ 8
Total	100	+10
Profit Change 1975-78		
1 year decline, 1 year increase	61.5	+ 6
2 year increase	38.5	+ 4
Total	100	+10
Average Net Profits % 1975-1978		
0-5	61.5	- 8
6-10	23.1	+23
21-25	15.4	- 5
Total	100	+10

In terms of average net profit percentage between 1975-78, high profitability did not seem to guarantee the creation of net new jobs. Therefore, the firm's track record should not be the only basis for evaluation. The firms with a record of moderate profitability were the only ones creating net new jobs.

b. Current Vacancies

Size of the Firm

In absolute terms, the smallest firms had the largest number of vacancies although the larger firms accounted for a greater relative share of vacancies. This finding appears to conflict with the earlier one that the smallest firms did not create the most net new jobs over the past year. This apparent conflict will be discussed below.

Table 18: Size of the Firm by Current Vacancies

Size of Firm	Vacancies					
	0	1-10	11-25	Total		
(employees)	Firms %	Firms %	Firms %	Firms %	Vacancies	%
1-25	88.2	76.5	-	82.7	85	54.5
26-50	4.4	8.8	-	5.8	8	5.1
51-100	7.4	2.9	50	6.7	21	13.5
over 100	-	11.8	50	4.8	42	26.9
Total	100	100	100	100	156	100

Performance

A large number of firms reporting losses in the financial year 1978-79 had many vacancies, as did firms reporting large profits. The performance of the firms cannot therefore be taken as a certain indication of their job creating potential, which again conflicts with earlier evidence that the firms with the largest profits created the most new jobs.

In terms of changes in turnover between 1975-78, the firms reporting a decline in one year and increase in one year, and those reporting an increase throughout the period had the most vacancies, although the former had relatively more vacancies. Unstable firms therefore had relatively the greatest potential for creating jobs, which confirms the earlier finding.

In terms of changes in profits, the firms showing a decline in profits in one year and an increase in the other - those firms which were relatively unstable - had the most vacancies.

c. The Employment of Local Residents

The creation of jobs for local residents should be distinguished from general employment creation - it is quite conceivable that local authorities may be asked to subsidise firms creating no or very few jobs for local residents because all or most employees commute into the area. It was shown earlier that only about one third of employees in the average firm lived within the borough, while one quarter of the firms employed no local residents at all. The research investigated the job creation potential of firms in respect of local residents.

Size of the Firm

It will be seen from Table 19 that the smallest firms (1-25 employees) employed the largest number of local residents in both absolute and relative terms. Of the firms employing from 61 to 100% of their workforce from residents in the local area, all were the smallest firms, accounting for 43.3% of all local jobs. However, the largest firms in the survey also made a substantial contribution (35.6%) to the employment of local residents. Since the survey was under-representative of the smallest firms, it is possible that they might have contributed an even greater proportion of local jobs than the table indicates. Although we know which firms created the most net new jobs and which employed the most local residents, the survey did not reveal which firms created the most local net new jobs, simply because such complexity would have meant examining the firms' employment records. Local authorities faced with this dilemma will therefore have to decide which they prefer - the employment of more local residents or the creation of more new jobs (and, by implication, more local jobs).

Table 19: Total and Local Employment by Size of Firm

	Numbers Employed by % of Local Residents Employed									
Size of Firm (employees)	None	1-10%	11-20%	21-40%	41-60%	61-80%	81-90%	91-100%	Total	%
1-25	136*	114	106	178	110	50	26	50	770	31.9
26-50	38	38	76	38	38	-	-	-	228	9.4
51-100	-	340	-	63	63	-	-	-	466	19.3
+ 100	-	380	-	570	-	-	-	-	950	39.4
Total	174	872	182	849	211	50	26	50	2414	100
				Local Employment						
1-25	-	6	16	54	56	35	22	48	237	43.3
26-50	-	2	12	12	19	-	-	-	45	8.2
51-100	-	19	-	19	32	-	-	-	70	12.8
+ 100	-	21	-	174	-	-	-	-	195	35.6
Total	-	48	28	259	107	35	22	48	547	100

*all figures are numbers of employees

Age of the Firm

Relatively more of the youngest firms (1-10 years) employed a higher proportion of local residents than older firms, although the differences were not very substantial. In addition, relatively fewer of the youngest firms employed no local residents at all. The combination of these two findings points to the youngest firms (1-10 years) having a greater impact on the creation of jobs for local residents.

Table 20: Age of Firm by Employment of Local Residents

Age in Years	Labour Living Locally None Firms %	1-40 Firms %	41-100 Firms %	Total Firms %
1-10	32	30.4	45.4	35.6
11-25	28	26.1	27.3	26.9
Over 25	40	43.5	27.3	37.5
Total	100	100	100	100

d. Linkages with the Market

Size of the Firm (turnover)

The smaller firms (turnover below £1m) had stronger linkages than larger firms with the marketplace within the borough, as well as within the West End, City and Greater London areas. Although the local market was more important to the smaller firms than to the larger firms, the difference was marginal. (Note: 18.3% of firms with an annual turnover below £1m stated that their major customers were located within the borough, while only 11.8% of the larger firms stated that the borough was their most important customer location.)

Table 21: Major Location of Customers by Annual Turnover

Turnover	Camden Firms %	West End & City Firms %	Rest of Gtr London Firms %	Outside Gtr London Firms %	Total Firms %
	Location				
Up to £1m	18.3	21	40.8	19.7	100
Over £1m	11.8	-	23.5	64.7	100
Total	17.0	17	37.5	28.4	100

Age of the Firm

The youngest firms (1-5 years old) were more dependent on the local market than older firms. Both the borough and the adjacent West End and City areas were more important to the youngest firms, while the rest of Greater London was more important to the older firms.

Table 22: Major Location of Customers by Age of the Firm

Age in Years	Camden Firms %	West End & City Firms %	Rest of Gtr London Firms %	Outside Gtr London Firms %	Total Firms %
	Location				
1-5	39.1	21.7	30.4	8.7	100
6-10	21.4	14.3	57.1	7.1	100
11-50	31.0	35.1	72.6	61.3	100
Over 50	13.3	13.3	26.7	46.7	100
Total	21.2	17.3	36.5	25.0	100

5. Linkages with Suppliers

Size of the Firm (turnover)

Although the smallest firms were more dependent on the rest of Greater London for their main suppliers, it was only the smallest firms which had any major suppliers in the borough.

Table 23: Major Location of Suppliers by Annual Turnover

Turnover	Camden Firms %	West End & City Firms %	Rest of Gtr London Firms %	Outside Gtr London Firms %	Total Firms %
	Location				
Up to £1m	28.6	4.3	44.3	22.8	100
Over £1m	-	17.6	17.6	64.7	100
Total	23.0	6.9	39.1	31.0	100

Age of the Firm

Again we see that the youngest firms (1-5 years) were most dependent on the rest of Greater London as the major location of their suppliers, although in the borough the youngest firms had the strongest linkages with their local suppliers.

Table 24: Major Location of Suppliers by Age of Firm

Age in Years	Location: Camden Firms %	West End & City Firms %	Rest of Gtr London Firms %	Outside Gtr London Firms %	Total Firms %
1-5	39.1	-	52.2	8.7	100
6-10	21.4	7.1	50.0	21.4	100
11-50	21.6	7.8	33.3	32.3	100
Over 50	-	13.3	46.7	40.0	100
Total	22.3	6.8	41.7	29.1	100

SUMMARY AND CONCLUDING REMARKS

The overall assistance criterion of seeking to maximise employment in the long run has been re-interpreted for the purposes of this survey. The three main questions to be answered are:

1. Which firms have tended to create the most net new jobs?
2. Which firms have tended to create the most jobs for local residents?
3. Which firms have shown the strongest linkages with the local economy (and, by implication, have generated the most local jobs)?

The findings of the survey provide a basis for establishing the criteria for assistance following these general questions. Several qualifying points need to be made. The findings may be peculiar to the borough from which the sample was chosen, although many of the characteristics of the area are to be found in other parts of London and, indeed, in the rest of the country. The extent to which the findings are of general applicability will therefore depend on where similar inner city characteristics are to be found. Because there were some unavoidable biases when selecting the sample, there may be distortions in the results which would make some of the conclusions invalid (or questionable). This weakness typifies most small business research, however, and it is hoped that the conclusions will at least be of interest even if not statistically pure.

The findings cannot easily be summarised in order to answer the three questions, although some valuable lessons and inferences can be drawn from the above tables. The findings are not clear about which firms created the most net new jobs, since in the previous year the largest firms in the sample created more jobs both absolutely and relatively than the smallest firms, although in terms of vacancies at the time of the interviews, the smallest firms (with fewer than 26 employees) had more openings than all the other firms in the sample combined. Although the smallest firms did not record the largest net job gains in the previous year, they were responsible for a significant share of the gains.

The findings are equally unclear about the financial performance of the firms in the sample and their employment creating potential. An examination of the recent histories of some of the firms indicates that considerable job gains were made by firms with unstable financial histories, and that moderate rather than outstanding profitability led to larger numbers of new jobs over the past year. In developing criteria for assistance, local authorities should not therefore overlook firms with unstable financial histories and, by inference, firms without a track record might themselves have considerable job creating potential.

There is greater clarity in the findings about the employment of local residents. The smallest and youngest (less than 10 years old) firms created absolutely more new jobs than the oldest firms, although the latter's contribution was still significant. By inference, new young firms and those in the start-up phase are likely to provide a large number of jobs for local residents. In the marketplace, too, the smallest and youngest firms had conclusively the strongest linkages with the local economy. Buying from and selling to other local firms would, of course, itself create external benefits in terms of employment creation.

In selecting firms for assistance, therefore, local authorities should not ignore the claims of the smallest firms: indeed, there is a strong case for those local authorities without small business policies and programmes to consider assisting small business as a way of maximising employment growth in the local economy.

6 Premises and the development of small firms

NICHOLAS FALK
URBED

INTRODUCTION

There is continuing controversy over how far local factors inhibit the birth and growth of small enterprise. Some argue that it is primarily lack of demand that holds back growth. The Wilson Committee stressed the difficulties small firms have in obtaining finance(1). The present government has heavily criticised the planning policies of local government(2). There is also a view that financial institutions, in avoiding investing in run-down urban areas, have held back the development of expanding firms(3). While there is some truth in all of these, reaching an agreement on the division of responsibilities between the public and private sectors has proved difficult because of the general lack of understanding of business dynamics.

The need to intervene in areas of high unemployment has led to government funding large factory building programmes, and claiming that these will create so many jobs. The involvement of large financial institutions in providing finance, with a public body taking the head lease, has not fundamentally changed the picture. There is something paradoxical about government providing substantial subsidies to large companies to go to areas of high unemployment while drawing away from anything that could be called a subsidy to small enterprise.

In order to see what form of intervention would best stimulate the growth of new enterprise, we found it necessary to devise a theory to explain the growth of small enterprises, which we then tested by drawing up case studies of the development of a cross-section of 15 companies. In this paper we first review the evidence for there being an unmet demand for small premises, before analysing the normal stages in the development of small firms, and the support required at each stage.

UNMET DEMAND

A series of surveys have shown that difficulties in obtaining premises are a major factor, not only in causing firms to leave inner city areas, but also in stopping those that remain from growing or operating efficiently(4). A new survey of 357 employers undertaken for the Department of the Environment shed considerable light on why firms vacate their premises. A number of conclusions can be drawn from the wealth of data in the survey(5).

(i) Movement is quite common within the same area. Twenty-five per cent of firms have moved in the past 5 years or are considering moving, and 7% have moved to their present inner city location within the last 5 years. Five per cent are looking for premises in the same area, and 90% move less than 10 miles. However, this falls to

72% in the case of those employing more than 50 persons, who accounted for 79% of the employees in the manufacturing sample.

(ii) The main reasons for considering moving involve the present premises. The five most important factors are suitability, comparative rent or purchase price, security of tenure, room for expansion, and loading facilities. Convenience of the location and availability of labour are also rated as particularly important.

(iii) The least satisfactory aspects of inner city locations are room for expansion, suitability and loading facilities, while the most satisfactory is price.

(iv) Thirty-three per cent of those who moved would have stayed if they could have altered their premises, 17% if they could have renegotiated their lease or bought their premises, and 9% if suitable labour had been available.

(v) The improvements requested by more than 10% of the firms were easier deliveries, lower rates, improved local services or environment, and better transport for employees.

(vi) Large firms (over 200 employees) differed from very small firms (under 50) in being more likely to own their own site (81% vs 47%), and in reporting a change of ownership in the last 10 years (40% vs 25% overall). Large firms also place much more importance on room for expansion, relationships with unions, labour costs, levels of rates and the availability of grants.

A study by Mason of firms relocating in Manchester found that over 15% of firms had changed location at least once within a period of less than 10 years(6). Sixty-three per cent relocated within the same area. A survey of firms in inner Leeds by Chalkley suggested that 'the majority of firms which moved from inner areas did so not through choice but because of the lack of suitable premises in central locations'(7).

Other evidence of the problems facing small firms comes from surveys of employers undertaken by local authorities, such as the London Borough of Southwark and Hammersmith(8), and from a series of articles in the Estate Times based on research carried out by URBED in 1976. Surveys of industrial estates showed that very little was provided for the relatively small firm. Although in inner London boroughs, for example, some 50% of manufacturing firms employ less than 10 people, and thus normally require under 5,000 sq ft (the average floor space per worker in manufacturing is 400 sq ft), very few units of less than 5,000 sq ft had been constructed. The reasons given by estate agents at the time were that financial institutions, who funded most new development, did not favour property let to small firms because of the management problems, while publicly subsidised factory provision in the assisted areas tended to make private development uneconomic.

The Coopers and Lybrand study commissioned by the Department of Industry and published in 1980 broadly confirmed these findings(9). It concluded that "a shortage of small industrial premises persists in the country as a whole ... there is clear evidence that the shortage of premises has constrained the establishment and development of small firms; the provision of premises on suitable terms has undoubtedly itself had the effect of stimulating the formation of new firms and the growth of existing small firms".

As a consequence of this evidence (and pressure from organisations like the Association of Independent Businesses), developers and public authorities have begun to build many more small units and, indeed, this is one of the few growing parts of the construction industry. But is there a danger, in the desire to meet a need rapidly, of producing an inappropriate product? The spectre of prefabricated high rise housing haunts many local authorities who had seen them originally as the answer to the 'housing crisis'. If anything, this danger has been magnified by the recent tax incentives for the development of small units.

For, though many firms complain of difficulties with obtaining suitable accommodation, the problem is to know what facilities to provide and where. Both the private and public sectors are worried about investing in the development of premises whose costs cannot be recovered. For example, a GLC committee report, Commercial and Industrial Development: a new approach, June 1978 argues:

> "An answer to the question "who is likely to want what?" is surely fundamental to London's strategy. Ideally, what needs to be established is the overall requirement of industry and commerce and how far the property known to be available or zoned or earmarked for the purpose (or which could be so arranged) will meet that demand. All the officers concerned have wrestled with this problem but so far without success. What frankly is lacking is the answer to the following fundamental questions: What is the foreseeable demand? And to what extent does the existing potential stock fail (if fail it does) to meet the demand?"(10)

One of the difficulties in assessing whether what is provided will meet demand is the difficulty of understanding what small firms really want. It is common to talk as though offices and factories are distinct building types, and manufacturing and service industry play distinct roles. Yet anyone who has had much dealings with firms who employ less than, say, 10 people, knows that they are extremely hard to categorise. For the very essence of a small firm is its flexibility, which requires it to do a 'bit of everything'.

STAGES OF DEVELOPMENT

While planners distinguish between the use made of the premises - a warehouse or a factory, for example - and the size of floor space, it is not normal to make distinctions in terms of the stage of development of the enterprise. Yet the requirements and resources available to the new entrepreneur may be totally different from a firm that has been established some years. In order to make better planning and design decisions, it is necessary to have some conceptual framework. The general theory we tested out through a number of case studies is that there are a series of stages in the normal life of a business roughly equivalent to those in the life of a human being. If we are right, then it seems reasonable to argue that the environment may either encourage or inhibit growth, depending on how appropriate it is to the stage of development.

a) Conceptual framework

We have termed the five stages: (i) embryonic, (ii) infant, (iii) growing up, (iv) established, (v) institutional

The embryonic stage is when the business is still an idea or a hobby. Most people start without much capital or confidence either. Hence they want to minimise their commitments and obtain the maximum support and encouragement. Where residential accommoation is plentiful, people often start in their garage, a spare room, or on the kitchen table. Their existing job provides security, while they try to establish the basis of a new business through 'moonlighting'.

The infant stage is when the business develops from a hobby or part-time interest into a venture that supports one or more self-employed people. It begins to own equipment, which takes up space, and a separate address may be required. A supportive environment is particularly important at this point, which is where clustering together with other related firms can be helpful. The infant can grow very quickly, and so scope for expansion is important, and this is often best provided in old buildings in run-down areas.

The growing up stage is one where the supportive environment becomes less important, as the firm can do more for itself. Instead of sharing resources, the firm wants to be able to own them. The firm now wants self-contained rooms with its own entrance. It may start employing people on production, instead of sub-contracting the work, which will require a better quality of premises if it is to attract and retain staff.

The established stage is the point where a certain level of inertia has been reached, and repeat orders enable the business to consider longer term questions, like owning their own premises. The need for easier access and a better image become important at this point.

The institutional stage is usually reached when the business becomes part of a group. At this point production often becomes divorced from administration, and the building begins to take on a symbolic as opposed to a functional purpose.

Because a series of stages can be defined it does not mean that businesses necessarily pass from one to another. Many firms, particularly those run by 'craftsmen', tend to remain personal businesses and avoid taking on greater obligations. Others try to grow and overstretch themselves. Our observation of businesses that have grown to the institutional stage leads us to believe that few start out with this in mind. Rather, it is a combination of pressure of demand for what they make, coupled with fortunate opportunities that enables them to grow.

A crucial element of our model is that at each stage of development there comes a point, a threshold, where the business will have to take on new commitments. It knows the key to success is keeping obligations and resources in balance. The longer it takes to obtain or get rid of surplus resources, the less likely it is that firms will expand to reach their market potential.

A favourable business climate is important in encouraging firms to cross threshholds. Just as the chrysalis only develops into a butterfly when the climate is favourable, so a firm is only likely to change the balance of its functions when the prospects look promising. It is likely that the climate is influenced as much by the attitudes of other businesses in a locality as by national circumstances.

In assessing what firms require from their premises at each stage, we have isolated three aspects: location, facilities and cost.

The location refers to where the premises are situated. We know from other research that most people start as close to home as possible. In our research we wanted to find out at which stage they were likely to locate in an inner city area.

The facilities refer to what the premises offer in the way of accommodation and supporting services. We were concerned to find out what space firms really needed, what they used it for and what quality of accommodation was required.

The cost refers normally to rental in relation to the tenure granted in return. There are, of couse, other costs of fitting out, heating and rates, but it is typically the rent which is uppermost in firms' minds when they start. We wanted to find out what firms expected and were prepared to pay for.

In order to test this general theory and throw some light on the kind of premises needed, URBED embarked on a series of research projects. As one element, a series of 15 case studies were drawn up of established manufacturing firms in London and Manchester to find what kind of premises they had used(11). The sample was selected to cover a range of industries, in each of which we tried to select both a craft based and a more opportunistic firm (see Table 1).

In size, turnover ranged from £20,000 for a 5 man business, to £3m for one employing 19 people. None of the firms less than 14 years old employed over 20, and all but 2 over this age employed more than 20. Only half were located in the inner city at the time of interview, but a number more had occupied space in inner city areas at some stage.

The case studies confirmed our hypothesis that firms passed through stages of growth, in which their requirements changed. Table 2 summarises the premises used at different stages in development, and Table 3 plots their development through different types of premises.

TABLE 1: CASE STUDIES

LONDON REGION FIRMS

CASE	INDUSTRY	DATE ESTAB	CURRENT EMPLOYMENT		LATEST TURNOVER	NO. OF PREMISES		BUSINESS DEVELOPMENT AND SPACE USE	SPIN OFF AND LANGUAGE
			FULL TIME	PART TIME		MAIN FACTORY	EXTENSIONS		
A	Electronics	1965	350	-	-	3 (+ sales unit out of London & Abroad)	4	Expanded to 450 in 1971 then contracted so had to dispose of one purpose-built extension	New firm about to start up (Inmos)
B	Electronics	1957	30	75	£230,000	4	1	Extensive use of out-workers reduced need for additional workspace	Survived major crisis
C	Furniture	1969	8	5	£ 90,000	1	1	Able to take over cheap space in situ as required	
D	Furniture	1968	5	1	£ 20,000	7	1	Spent much of this period working on his own and living in a Welsh commune	Now is partner of a second firm and from whom he sub-contracts work
E	Clothing	1944	14	6	-	3		Employment rose to 24 in 1963 then reduced as more design incorporated	Links with another men's tailor, with which one of their directors is also concerned
F	Clothing	1959	70	-	£380,000	3	2	Currently expanding turnover by using new technology	First attempt failed
G	Craft	1957	90+	-	£1,900.00	3 (+ 2 abroad)	2	Complex series of take-overs in 1969-75 brought in accom.	Respondant started another firm and left because of disagreement with partner
H	Craft	1920's	32	-	£350,000	6	1	Worked at home during World War II	
I	Design	1971	16	2	£150,000	4	2	Shared space with design firm	
J	Design	1969	9	3	£ 80,000	2	1	Worked from home for 7 years	
GREATER MANCHESTER FIRMS									
L	Engineering	1964	70		£9,000,000	2		Both premises obtained very cheaply as out of use and in bad state of repair	
M	Printing	1973	3		£ 71,000	2		In early period machine only purchased and used for nominal rent in previous owners space	
N	Clothing	1971	19		£3,000,000	2		Started from agency business, now producing clothes in Hong Kong for distribution to four continents	One partner previously distributed photographic goods
O	Distribution	1966	5	5	£100,000	1	1	Agency business requires no capital and minimum of space	Now developing own manufacturing business
P	Service	1968	120		£2,000,000	3	4	Started by university lecturers using garage in evenings	

TABLE 2: ACCOMMODATION OF CASE STUDY FIRMS

ACCOMMODATION AT THE INFANT STAGE

REGION	LOCATION	FIRM	AGE OF BUILDING	TYPE OF BUILDING	SPACE TYPE	SQ FT PER EMPLOYEE	£ RENT PER SQ FT
	Rural	A	Older	Factory	Large Single	50	
	Inner City	B	Older	House	Small Repetitive	100	
	Inner City	C	Older	House	Small Repetitive	250	0.10
	Inner City	D	Older	Warehouse	Mixed	400	0.30
SOUTH	Inner City	E	Older	Factory	Large Single	69	0.22
EAST	Suburban	F	Older	Shop	Small Repetitive	33	
	Inner City	G	Older	Shop	Small Repetitive	50	
	Inner City	H	Older	Warehouse		80	3.00
	Inner City	J	Older	House	Small Repetitive	250	
	Centre	K	Older	Shop	Large Single	167	
	Inner City	L	Older	Factory		400	0.10
	Inner City	M	Older	Mill	Large Single	333	0.75
NORTH	Inner City	N	Older	Warehouse	Large Single	225	
WEST	Rural	P	Older	Shop	Small Repetitive	86	0.83
	Inner City	Q	Older	Mill	Mixed	500	0.25

ACCOMMODATION AT INTERVIEW

	Inner City	A	Older	Factory	Mixed	108	0.66
	New Town	B	Modern	Factory	Mixed	155	
	Inner City	C	Older	Warehouse	Large Rep.	333	0.40
	Inner City	D	Older	Warehouse	Large Rep.	333	0.33
	Inner City	E	Modern	Factory	Large Rep.	90	0.94
SOUTH	Suburban	F	Modern	Factory	Large Single	57	
EAST	Central	G	Older	Shop	Mixed	80	
	Central	H	Older	Warehouse	Mixed	365	2.39
	Inner City	J	Older	Shop	Small Rep.	318	
	Central	K	Older	Office	Large Rep.	111	4.00
	Inner City	L	Older	Factory	Mixed	549	
NORTH	Inner City	M	Older	Mill	Large Single	333	0.75
WEST	Inner City	N	Modern	Factory	Mixed	316	
	Rural	P	Older	Shop	Small Rep.	86	0.83
	Suburban	Q	Modern	Factory	Mixed	433	

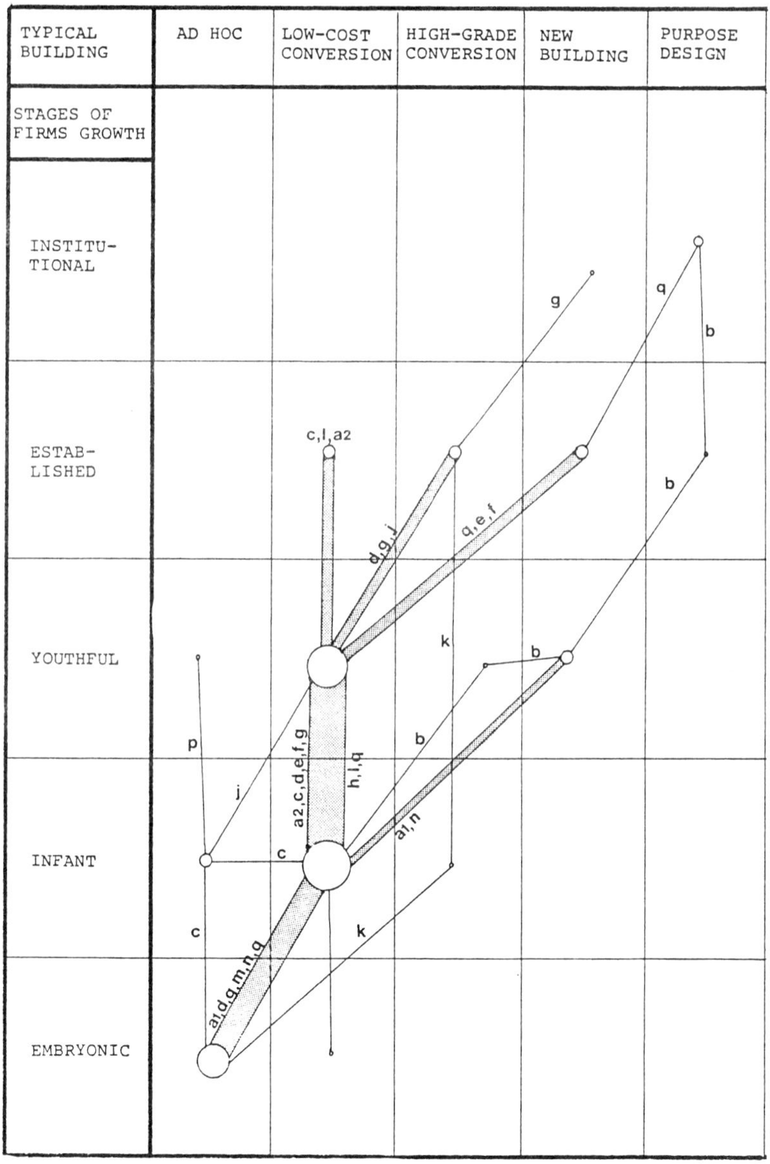

The hypothesis tested was that each stage in a firm's growth is associated with a particular standard of building: embryonic firms using 'ad hoc' space, infant firms using low-cost conversions etc. The diagram shows that all the firms interviewed departed from this model at some time in their history; eg. Q, E and F stayed in low-cost conversions throughout their growing-up period, and moved directly into new buildings once they were fully established, without passing through any high-grade conversion.

b) Starting out

We found, as expected, that most businesses did not start in their own premises, but went through a period of 'incubation' in which the founders were working part-time on their business idea and supporting themselves with other types of employment. Only one-third of the entrepreneurs we interviewed set up right away as infant firms. Of those that did, one had a post-war 'demob' gratuity, and another a large redundancy payment. Two others began with consultancies, having already had experience of the industry concerned. The final one had previously set up a firm that failed, and so he felt he knew how to go about it the second time.

The remaining two thirds of our sample, which included a firm which suffered near collapse and had to start again by borrowing a corner of a friend's factory for two-and-a-half years, all went through what we call the 'embryonic' stage.

i) Location In their early stage, the firms seized local trading opportunities located near the founder's home. Nearly half felt tied to the location for commercial reasons. At this stage most were located in a village, a small country town, or a suburban area of a large city. The only firms to start in an older inner city area were ones that did so in the entrepreneur's home.

ii) Facilities Five of the 11 respondents used their own homes as a base for their prospective businesses. While in one case only one room was used, in most cases work was spread throughout the house. It is perhaps not surprising that none lived in a new house at the time.

Other premises were the basement of a pub, a garage, a mews, a converted warehouse and part of another firm's factory space. Thus all the businesses used 'ad hoc' premises in a rough and ready condition, which they adapted to their needs. On average, 2 people were involved at this stage, and they typically used an area of 350 sq ft, which is equivalent to one-third of a modern terraced house, and a great deal smaller than the average so-called 'nursery' unit.

iii) Cost Rental varied widely at this stage, the extremes being free accommodation at home and an annual sum paid by the 'restart' firm for part of another firm's factory. At this stage it is not pounds per square foot but total outgoings that firms look at, and the less they have to provide for themselves, the more can be spent on building up the business. Tenure tends to be on a 'grace and favour' basis, and few are likely to contemplate taking on a lease at this stage.

c) The growing up stage

Most of the firms interviewed took between 10 and 15 years to grow up and reach a threshold of security. During this period they changed their accommodation 3 to 5 times. Forty-seven different main premises were mentioned and 22 branches. The 15 firms interviewed had been in existence from between 6 and 60 years, and ranged in size from 3 to 120 employees.

i) Location It is at the infant stage that firms begin to set up on their own. Locational ties are strong, with two-thirds emphasising access to labour and one-third emphasising access to markets and suppliers. All but 3 were located at this stage in inner city areas, and there was no noticeable difference between firms in London and Manchester. Entrepreneurs tried to strike a balance between proximity to their own homes, and locations which their staff could reach easily. Analysis of the numbers of small manufacturing firms in different parts of London shows how the older industrial areas not only have more small firms, but also higher birth rates.

ii) Facilities None of the 15 firms occupied modern premises at the infant stage, and only 3 used premises originally designed as factories. Four occupied converted shops, 3 converted warehouses, 3 converted houses and 2 former mills. This suggests that planning use categories are not matched to the requirements of the new firm. What firms occupied were typically what we have called low-cost conversions, where the minimum had been spent on making the building habitable.

The infant firms employed 11 people each on average in the space of 1800 sq ft, which is much more intensive use of space than mature firms (two-thirds the level of all the firms studied), and ranging between 50 and 500 sq ft per person.

The premises occupied a variety of types of space. Five were larger single spaces, 6 were small repetitive spaces, and 2 were mixed. The floor plans of how firms use their space show that requirements are far more varied than is usually conceived in modern buildings. Half had no ground floor space, which was a higher proportion than the established firms, suggesting that upper stories of old buildings are accepted more readily by young firms (a point which is confirmed by studies we have done of the occupants of multi-storey buildings(12).

iii) Costs The rental information available shows only one exception from the range of between £0.10 and £0.83 per sq ft per annum. These costs are those reported for the times at which they were paid and are thus much lower than those paid by the same firms later in their growth. There is no way of standardising this information, but it would be unwise to disregard it, as leases often allow companies to continue paying 'historic' low rents for many years.

DESIGN REQUIREMENTS

If demand for small premises exceeds supply, there is a major question of what should be supplied to fill the gaps, and who should organise and finance it. We have seen how most firms grow up in older premises in inner city areas, change their premises quite frequently, and use them for a range of purposes. Yet financial institutions prefer to invest in new buildings in secure locations, let to occupants who are likely to remain for the period of the lease, and use their premises for a single defined purpose. Leases are designed to preserve the landlord's investment, and usually restrict sub-letting or moving. The new firm is discouraged by the requirement to produce three years' trading records or a personal guarantee.

While it should not be too difficult to design new units that meet small firms' requirements, surveys suggest that current designs are often deficient. A major survey by the Centre for Advanced Land Use Studies (CALUS) found that 77% of small firms considered their particular location important (and hence would prefer to stay where they are if they could obtain suitable premises), but most were critical of what was provided(13).

Many firms when they are growing up do not need the image of being on a modern industrial estate and, indeed, for some it can be quite inappropriate. Nor do most need high spaces (8 out of 15 firms we interviewed had no space over 12ft high). However, they do need somewhere that a vehicle can park, and want their premises to be sound and secure.

The CALUS study was highly critical of modern speculative units. Firms complained about features like defective doors, leaking roofs and a general lack of attention to security and heating costs. Table 4 presents some conclusions from several studies.

TABLE 4: COMPARISON OF CASE STUDIES WITH PREVIOUS RESEARCH

	CALUS SURVEY FIRMS USING PREMISES BUILT SINCE 1958* Manufacturing & Warehousing Firms		AJ STUDY FLATTED FACTORY IN EAST LONDON**	AJ STUDY NURSERY UNITS MILTON KEYNES**	REGENERATION LTD SURVEY OF WOOLWICH REDEVELOPMENT FACTORY**		CASE STUDIES**
	All Firms	Small Firms			New Units	Rehab. Units	
No of respondents	173	31	12	4	4	10	15
Average floor area	Up to 30,000ft²	Up to 5,000ft²	2,270ft²	500ft²	29,4000ft²	8,685ft²	13,175ft²
Average Workforce	47	14	28	2	39	15	53
Use of upper fls.	9% accept 20% upper stores level	6% accept 13% upper stores level	75% no ground level space	All ground level	All ground level	80% no ground level space	36% no ground level space
Need for clean internal height	Most frequent response 16' - 20'	Most frequent response 16' - 20'	10ft	10ft	15ft	12ft	53% no space over 12ft.
Need for external handstanding	51%	35%	joint use	joint use	exclusive use	joint use	60% have own external space
Car Parking spaces	average 18	average 11	joint use	joint use	exclusive use	joint use	53% have own car park
Commercial vehicle traffic	82% less than 10 vehicles per day	87% less than 5 vehicles per day	-	-	average 19 vehicles per day	average 4 vehicles per day	
Commercial ties to location	firms for whom location is important	firms for whom location is important					33%
Labour ties to location	74%	74%					

* Ogden, Christine., Buildings for Industry (Centre for Advanced Land Use Studies, 1979)
** Unpublished studies by Martin Symes, University of London

While none of the design factors is likely to inhibit the growth of a small firm, they are all irritations which could help make the entrepreneur's life easier if they were removed. Furthermore, the appearance of many industrial estates, as well as main roads in inner city areas, gives an impression of industry being messy and old fashioned. There is evidence that this helps to create an unfavourable attitude in the minds of young people and women, which makes it harder for small firms that are growing to attract staff. While many of the problems of a dilapidated appearance may well stem from the occupants, careful planning and design could enable unsightly piles of materials to be screened. Better estate management should extend to the provision of signing and the maintenance of common parts, like pavements and parking areas.

Finally, it should be recognised that some firms are quite happy with an inferior environment, providing they can keep their costs down. It is surprising how many successful firms started in barns. Furthermore, high technology is perfectly compatible with old buildings. Both the Digital Equipment Corporation in the USA and Sinclair Radionics in the UK are based in former mills. A survey we undertook for the OECD showed that firms are more concerned wth matters such as whether the rubbish is collected or whether the roads and pavements are properly maintained, than with appearances, except in situations where it is important to impress customers(14). Indeed, many new firms would oppose environmental improvements that threatened to lead to rises in rent or rates, or to attract officialdom! This particularly applies to firms involved in repairing or recycling old equipment who need yard space(15).

PLANNING IMPLICATIONS

While the case studies are an admittedly small sample, together with other studies they enable a fairly clear picture to be drawn concerning the premises that are required, and the implications for planning if constraints are to be removed. We have summarised these below.

a) Provide range of premises

Because businesses change rapidly, as a result of demand, it is essential that premises are equally adaptable. In the early stages it is best to be able to expand or contract at the same address, and this is one advantage of sharing a large old building. Because of the importance of retaining staff, firms need a range of premises in each locality, forming the equivalent of a series of rungs on a ladder. Table 3, which plots the development of the firms we interviewed, shows how there is a definite progression from 'ad hoc' space, through typically a low cost conversion to either a high grade conversion (with heating, decoration, etc) or a new building. Variations in facilities and cost are as important as variations in size to enable a smooth progression to be made. A wider range of premises could help firms in surviving ups and downs. For, if too much space has to be taken on, the firms can be over-extended if business slumps. Conversely, too little space leads to cramped conditions and inefficiency. Planners should try to establish gaps, which can be filled in new developments, and should encourage schemes which are easily modified over time.

b) Be flexible over use

The very small firm typically fills a specialised niche, but performs a range of functions. Hence space is required that can be turned to a variety of uses. The floor plans of the firms we looked at show they typically had a reception area, an office, a workshop or production area, stores, a canteen, and sometimes research, library or meeting room space as well. It is often, therefore, somewhat arbitrary as to what to call a small firm's premises. A further complication is that activities like design studios or some forms of higher technology manufacturing, like electronics, require space that is as comfortable as an office, and do not require high floor loadings or ceiling heights. Yet the rules applied both in development control and in institutional investment tend to result in single purpose premises that are inflexible and unsuited to the requirements of most small firms. Planners should stop bothering about the use of smaller units and concentrate on ensuring there is sufficient spare capacity.

c) Provide an appropriate environment

Though premises to a planner or investor are largely seen as bricks and mortar, to an occupant they represent an environment which extends beyond the walls. Factors such as the availability of supporting services and helpful neighbours are as important to the small firm as to the household equirements, however, differ greatly, depending on both the orientation of the entrepreneur and the type of industry. The 'craft oriented' businesses we studied were typically more likely to stay the same size, and did so either by rejecting or deferring orders or sub-contracting work. Consequently the availability of other similar businesses in the locality is important to their survival. Independence is greatly valued, and such firms will often prefer their own premises, however run-down, to fitting in to somewhere that has been planned. Because very small businesses have neither the time nor resources to seek out professional advice, it is usually far better for them to be in close contact with other similar businesses whom they can draw on for advice and specialist services. As most goods are moved by van or car, rather than truck, many of the locational considerations that apply to warehousing, for example, are irrelevant. There is, therefore, an inconsistency between the locations and premises that suit small firms as they are growing up, and what financial institutions choose to invest in. Investors should stop using criteria that are irrelevant to the small firm, like proximity to motorways, and instead direct investment where most firms are concentrated already, which means investing in the apparently riskier older inner city area.

BUSINESS LIFE CYCLE

a) Embryonic

Most businesses start in a part-time way to minimise the risk and finance involved. People often begin in a garage or spare room. However, in inner city areas such space is scarce. Hence there is a demand in residential areas for places where people can use equipment and obtain advice. Sometimes this is provided by an adult education institute. It can form part of the role of a community workshop, like the Ormond Road Craft Centre in North Islington. Where the community workshop forms part of a complex of workshops, like the one run by the Frobisher Adult Education Institute at Hope (Sufference) Wharf,

Rotherhithe, or the 'open workshop' at Clerkenwell Workshops, it can provide a taste of the world of work, and encouragement for people to start up in business on their own.

b) Infant

The next stage is for the business to develop from a hobby or part-time interest into an independent firm supporting one or more people. At this stage the business needs an address which is close to home, as long hours will be worked. This may be no more than a place to receive messages and perhaps visitors. However, many people at this stage welcome the chance of sharing premises and support services with someone else.

One approach is to license part of somebody else's premises, perhaps a firm that is contracting, or that has taken on spare space for future expansion. There are also a growing number of 'working communities' that cater especially for the tiny firm. Perhaps the best known examples are Barley Mow Workspace in Chiswick and 5 Dryden Street in Covent Garden, where desk space can be rented, and where the open-plan layout appeals to design related firms. The services may range from reception to business advice and, for example, Clerkenwell Workshops has an arrangement with City University Business School to draw on students for consultancy and help.

The advantages of the working community at this stage are basically that the firm can obtain more than it could afford on its own. There is the possibility of expanding without moving address. Collaboration is easier, and there is less isolation than would otherwise face the new firm. The working community concept could apply to an industry like clothing; for example, there is a garment centre in Philadelphia, which may provide a useful model. Another variant is a technology centre linked to a university or polytechnic, like Enterprise Lancaster.

As well as space in converted buildings, it is also important to provide small spaces for firms that create noise or handle heavy materials. In light engineering or car repair, what is wanted is often a superior kind of lock-up garage, available on a short lease, which could often be located on patches of waste ground adjoining a converted building. The 'start-up' units would be an excellent temporary use for land that may eventually be redeveloped, providing 'instant workspace', rather like pre-fab houses did after the last war.

c) Growing up

Once the firm has been in business a few years, and starts to grow, its needs change. It may well want a self-contained space with a separate entrance. Furthermore, a better standard of premises may be required to attract and retain staff. It is still perfectly possible to use an old building, by taking on a floor. Our research suggests that at this stage firms that start in the suburbs may move into the inner city to take advantage of 'second-hand' premises and pools of experienced labour. An enterprise park forming part of a larger industrial estate could help make business easier by enabling complementary firms to share overheads without losing their individual identities.

Alternatively, the firm may go for a more independent space, such as a railway arch or a shop, particularly if it is important to be within easy reach of customers. Another possibility is to take on a small building with several other firms.

d) Established

Once firms reach a certain size and age they begin to look around for more suitable premises. This particularly applies where a lease has to be renewed, or a major expansion is planned. The need for easier access for heavy goods vehicles and space for growth becomes more important. At this stage, purpose-built industrial estates become attractive. Firms often have to move away to the suburbs of a new and expanded town, because they cannot find anywhere suitable within the locality. Yet complexes of buildings can be turned into perfectly attractive industrial estates as the Westminster Bunting development of the old AEI Works at Woolwich provides. There is also considerable scope for redeveloping wasteland sites that would be unsuitable for other uses, such as alongside railway lines or docks.

Alternatively, an established company could well acquire a medium sized vacant building, where it could combine all its activities. Many old buildings when refurbished can provide attractive looking premises. The firm can retain some space for expansion (and a good source of income) by sub-letting part to less established businesses.

Many businesses never grow beyond the embryonic stages, particularly where they are run by the 'craftsman' type of businessman. However, a very few eventually reach the point where they become 'institutions'. At this stage everyone will be interested in helping them!

DEVELOPMENT IMPLICATIONS

Now that so much is known about the need to provide a wider range of premises, if the growth of small enterprise is not to be artificially constrained, it is important to identify the factors that hold back the supply of what is required. Our research has identified a range of alternative models, and up and down the country initiatives are being launched which offer some hope. The big question is whether we are providing what is required on a large enough scale.

Discussions with developers and financial institutions point to three main difficulties which are restraining development:

a) Obtaining sites

It is still hard to obtain suitable sites that can be developed without substantial clearance costs and investment in infrastructure. Disagreement over valuation, and the fact that land is often owned by those who lack the resources to develop it, restricts supply. Then delays in installing services together with the complexities of securing the agreement of the many authorities involved, help to explain why Slough Estates say it takes twice as long to develop the same sized factory in Britain as in other countries(16).

b) Cutting costs

While building costs can rapidly escalate, what occupants are prepared to pay is more restricted. Rising energy, material and building costs make new buildings expensive. Yet refurbishment, unless it is carried out in an appropriate way, often does not lead to the expected savings. The need for an appropriate approach emerged from a study we did for the Department of the Environment/Hackney/Islington Partnership, in which we found over 25 instances of buildings being converted into small units, totalling over one million square feet and in most cases the cost of conversion was very low (under £5/sq ft)(17). Where the local authority was involved costs were very much higher. Our feasibility studies showed that reuse was not economically viable given the prices building owners were asking, unless an entrepreneurial approach was adopted which kept costs to a minimum.

c) Finding good tenants

No landlord wants to be bothered with troublesome tenants who create a mess, or do not pay the rent promptly. Yet inevitably most small businesses are marginal in their nature, and are run by independent minded people. The typical people employed to manage buildings and industrial estates have little sympathy for these kinds of occupant. Furthermore, rules regarding covenants and previous trading records rule out many tenants who desperately need space.

While there is no simple answer to these problems, we believe the answer lies in a partnership between the public and private sectors, in which entrepreneurial developers are encouraged to initiate and manage schemes that are more complex than large institutions can comfortably handle. It should be possible to find people with an interest in small business who can then manage complexes like working communities or enterprise parks in ways that encourage business development. Instead of surveyors, we need to draw on business graduates and company executives who are looking for new jobs.

PROMOTION OF TECHNOLOGY BASED ENTERPRISE

The environment needed for business to grow rapidly varies not only with the stage of the business, but also with the kind of business. As technology improves, the relative importance of different resource inputs changes. Whereas the first industrial revolution was dependent on easy access to cheap materials, energy and large markets, what is called the second industrial revolution is far more dependant on access to knowledge(18). This is seen at its extreme in electronics where we talked to those concerned with locating the microprocessor plants of INMOS and GEC/Fairchild. In this business continual innovation makes it vital to set up in areas which are most attractive to skilled engineers. The residential environment is just as important as the working environment, and explains the growth of what is known in the USA as the 'sunbelt'. But while the development of prototypes and the production of high value added items takes place in the same location, mass production fabrication will then be carried out wherever in the world reliable labour is cheapest or where government grants provide sufficient cash incentives. Hence high technology industry does not necessarily bring all that much direct employment.

The destructive effects of rapid technological change are very familiar to all the cities which developed as industrial centres in the 19th Century. Local authorities are therefore attempting to encourage industries that are based on new technologies, and to exploit the considerable resources of Britain's technologically oriented universities and polytechnics. This is particularly evident in the new interest in copying the American idea of science parks and innovation centres. Thus science parks have already been set up in Cambridge, Edinburgh and Warrington, and there has been an unsuccessful attempt at Peterlee(19). Others are planned or are under discussion in the Wirral in Merseyside, West London (linked to Brunel University), Bristol, Salford and Glasgow. Innovation centres have been formed or are under serious discussion in Birmingham, Strathclyde and Newcastle, and no doubt many other cities.

While it is encouraging that more consideration is being given to ways of applying technology to create new jobs, we have found considerable ignorance about the nature of technology-based enterprise and how to encourage it. An article in The Estates Times in July 1980 stated that 'in keeping with the image of Central Wirral, one of the most important recent proposals has been for a new Science Park on about 50 acres of council-owned land at Upton. The council hopes to attract a wide range of research/scientific/computer-based factories and offices, while retaining a clean environment'. We suspect that many local authorities are casting around wildly, and hoping to catch fish that are not only rare, but which are also likely to run through their nets.

There is a tendency to follow fads, without much regard to the conditions under which ideas are likely to succeed, or the scale required to achieve the desired results. Over the past 5 years URBEB has put forward a number of ideas which have been taken up. In 1975, a Fabian Pamphlet on the Inner City, argued for the creation of industrial parks in landscaped settings(20). A paper to the London Looks Forward Conference in 1977 advocated the use of industrial housing associations to provide rented premises(21). A pamphlet in 1978 entitled Think Small argued for setting up enterprise centres to provide supporting services(22). While ideas like these have won acceptance among planners and politicians, who in turn put pressure on financial institutions, there is a danger that the very organisations to whom these ideas appeal are unsuited to carrying them out. To establish what kind of environment technology-based enterprises require, URBED carried out a number of small studies. These included discussions with several leading technology-based enterprises in South East London, a survey of the interest of engineers in starting new companies, interviews with people concerned with the location of the INMOS,and GEC/Fairchild microprocessor plants, and a review of US experience with science parks and the promotion of innovation. The evidence we collected points to a number of conclusions that policy-makers need to recognise.

Where the objective is to create more viable long-term jobs then it is vital to build on the existing industrial structure as there are too few mobile plants and too many competing locations to rely on attracting investment from outside. The USA has successfully maintained the highest living standards in the world by not only increasing productivity but also, more importantly, by increasing the number employed in manufacturing. In the period 1959/73, this rose by 4m or 25%, when ours declined by 300,000. Most of this extra employment came from small, independent businesses, many of which 'spun-off' from large firms in order to 'do things their own way'.

Our analysis of the differences between the USA and Britain leads us to believe that their relative success was not only due to a more entrepreneurially minded culture, but also to far wider ranging programmes of public support, which reinforced each other. Thus many electronics firms in the 'sunbelt' were able to obtain vital contracts through preferential procurement schemes, and to tap into the enormous space and defence programmes of the 1960's. Seen in this context, developments like Science Parks and Innovation Centres were simply physical manifestations of an economic process and not causes of development.

The Americans have appreciated that the new enterprise, whether technologically based or not, is fairly indifferent to its surroundings, but is greatly concerned about contacts with customers and suppliers. Both universities and financial institutions have identified more closely with the economic development of their local communities, so that the general environment is conducive to growth. Established businesses locate where it is easiest to recruit highly qualified engineers. This in turn is linked to the proximity to a leading university, and the availability of a superior living environment. Good working conditions then form part of a package which companies can use to entice the people they want to work for them.

Furthermore, the physical factors that architects, planners and surveyors bother about, are often only a secondary part of the working environment(23). For example, at the RAND Corporation in Santa Monica, 24 hour access is important because many researchers lie on the beach during the day and work at night!

While there are some 80 Science Parks in the USA, their total direct employment is only 142,000 in some 2,000 firms. Nevertheless, if the basic environment is favourable, the experience of 'Silicon Valley' around Stanford University shows that an industrial park can be an important catalyst for local economic development. There the development of a science park on university-owned land provided space for businesses to set up that employed Stanford graduates, and who in turn supported the development of that university into one of the leading centres of technology in the world(24).

The success of the Stanford Industrial Park does not stem from the design and layout of the buildings so much as the drive of the person who conceived it, the former head of the university's engineering school. Correspondingly, the failure of a proposal for a science park in Birmingham to get off the ground lies we believe in the failure of the local authorities and consultants employed to enlist the support of a suitable 'driving force', and in their inability to adapt a basic idea to local circumstances.

Despite the importance of science parks, it is significant that two of the leading American producers of micro-computers (along with most new enterprises) started in cheap, second-hand premises, (Apple using a garage and Digital part of an old mill). In contrast, entrepreneurs' existing residence will determine the area of location. Where a new location is sought, as in the case of microprocessor firms, we discovered that the first consideration for the new business (INMOS) was attracting top engineers, which drew them to Bristol. In contrast, for the institutionalised business (GEC/Fairchild), the main factors were the availability of government grants and a local authority that would provide a suitable site quickly which drew them to a Special Development Area in Cheshire.

What is the scope for stimulating more people to 'spin-off' from established companies? In Europe, unlike the USA, it is rare for people from universities to set up companies to exploit their ideas. We found that though inner city areas often contain companies whose success depends on innovation (like Molins and Elliot Automation in the London Borough of Lewisham), they have such difficulties in attracting graduate engineers because it is a relatively expensive or unattractive place to live compared with the alternatives. As a consequence, the more innovative work (and consequently people) is concentrated in newer areas, or country towns. Thus inner city areas end up with few people with the will or capability to set up on their own. This suggests that more than just premises are needed to encourage technologically minded people to set up on their own.

MANAGEMENT IMPLICATIONS

considerable body of knowledge now exists about the nature of innovation and entrepreneurship, which we have tried to link to the less understood subject of physical development. Our research leads us to the overall conclusion that much more attention needs to be given to conceiving schemes or projects that are linked to the particular resources of an area, and to providing the kind of management that is appropriate. For example, in Newcastle great efforts are being made to attract electronics firms, whereas coal extraction and marine technology, where the area has a comparative advantage, seem to be being neglected We therefore conclude that three ingredients are required for successfully encouraging technologically-based enterprise at the local level.

a) <u>Simplify the task of running a new enterprise</u>

The entrepreneur's scarcest resource is time; consequently the easier it is to find what he needs, the greater the chances of early success. This particularly applies to businesses that are operating on the frontiers of science. We believe that in addition to technologically oriented working communities, whether in new or old buildings, a new approach to estate management is required that goes beyond collecting the rent and keeping the premises in good repair, to the provision of advice and the organisation of collaborative ventures. For example, there is also scope for developing simple computerised accountancy and other systems, combining these with 'hardware' like copying machines in technology centres. A major computer company is already doing this in the USA.

b) Undertake 'social audits' to mobilise under-utilised resources

Our review of ways in which colleges can encourage local economic development has exposed a far wider 'menu' of alternatives than most planners ever consider. We believe it is vital not only to engage the interest of people at the top of universities and polytechnics, but also to develop procedures for uncovering interest lower down, and relating under-utilised resources to the needs of local industry(25).

c) Build an environment which encourages enterprise

If our older industrial areas are to compete with the smaller towns and villages, it is vital that more effort is put into creating a total environment in which people want to 'live, work and play'. The large areas of waste land in our cities, such as former docks and railway marshalling yards, could provide the space; we have set out elsewhere how these can be turned into the kinds of 'urban villages' which will attract the young, able people who come to cities to be trained(26). These ideas have been taken up in some of the proposals put forward for the development of London's Surrey Docks. Creating new centres of activity is difficult anywhere, and particularly so in areas which suffer from the debris left by industry closing down. Hence, we believe it is essential to set up organisations that can not only attract and spend the necessary finance efficiently, but can do so with the degree of flair needed to make the most of any investment. Showmanship is needed to put the spotlight on achievements and to conceal the defects during the period of transition involved in turning a 'dying' into a 'thriving' economy.

REFERENCES

1. The Financing of Small Firms, Interim Report of the Committee to Review the Functioning of Financial Institutions, Cmnd 7503 HMSO, 1979.

2. See, for example, speech by Michael Heseltine at the Guildhall.

3. Industrial Estates and the Small Firm URBED, 1976.

4. Falk, Nicholas, 'Small Firms in the Innter City' in Policy Issues in Small Business Research, Gibbs, A and Webb, T (eds) Saxon House, 1980.

5. Industrial Facts and Forecasting Limited, Industry and Employment in the Inner City DoE, 1980.

6. Mason, P, 'Industrial decline in Greater Manchester 1966-75: a components of change approach', Urban Studies, Vol 17, No 11.

7. Mason, ibid.

8. Industrial Survey, London Borough of Southwark Planning Department, 1976. Industrial and Commercial Survey, London Borough of Hammersmith.

9. Coopers and Lybrand, The Provision of Premises for Small Firms Department of Industry, 1980.

10. Report to Employment Committee, GLC, 1978.

11. Case study fieldwork conducted by Martin Symes during 1979, in conjunction with DEGW, Architects, of Welbeck Street with assistance of a grant from the Gatsby Foundation. Symes, M (December 1979) Accommodation for Entrepreneurs (unpublished).

12. Church, V, Worthington, J, Eley, P and Symes, M, 'Use of Redundant Buildings: 35 Case Studies' Architects Journal, Vol 170, No 34, pp 387-403.

13. Building for Industry Centre for Advanced Land Use Studies, 1979.

14. Business Confidence and the Urban Environment OECD, 1979.

15. Tym, R and the Franklin Stafford Partnership, Back of the Yards, report for the DoE Docklands Partnership 1980.

16. Industrial Investment - a case study in factory buildings Slough Estates, 1979.

17. Space to Work, report for the DoE/Hackney/Islington Partnership URBED, 1980.

18. Falk, N, Think Small: Enterprise and the Economy Fabian Society, 1978.

19. Linking the College and the Community: Fostering New Enterprise URBED, 1977.

20. Falk, N and Martinos, H, Inner City: local government and economic renewal Fabian Society, 1975.

21. First steps in Regenerating London's Economy, Thames TV 'London Looks Forward' Conference, 1976 available from URBED.

22. Falk 1978 op cit.

23. 'The Working Environment', Built Environment, Vol 5, No 1 1979.

24. URBED 1977 op cit.

25. Linking the College and the Community: a practical guide URBED, 1980.

26. 'New Uses for Waste Land', Built Environment, Vol 4, No 4. See also Nicholas Falk in Encylopedia of the 21st Century, ed Allaby, M Macmillan, 1980.

7 Small firms in Britain and Europe: the perceived environment

DAVID WATKINS and TONY MORTON
Manchester Business School

INTRODUCTION

This paper summarises a research study designed to probe and compare the business perceptions of two interacting groups. On the one hand, owner-managers of small manufacturing enterprises (SMEs) and, on the other, managers of those financial institutions (FIs), particularly clearing banks, whose role it is to finance their businesses. In the case of SMEs, the retail, service and construction sectors were excluded from the study and the manufacturing sectors chosen were those in which businesses employing more than 10 but less than 200 people accounted for more than 25% of sector net output. Thus the SME focus was that of economically significant small manufacturing firms.

The chosen research design was to send matched postal questionnaires to randomly drawn samples from each group in each of 3 countries.

In this paper the authors will avoid detailed reference to the questionnaires used and severely restrict reference to the numerical data obtained (or the paper would be too long and too complicated to follow without continuous reference to the questionnaires.) A version of the full study is available from the senior author(1); here we are concerned with overall results which summarise analyses of 6 data sets in English, French and German obtained from more than 600 respondents.

The questionnaires sent to each national sub-group were carefully matched through a translation/retranslation procedure and individual piloting. More than two thirds of the questions on the SME questionnaires had directly equivalent questions on the FI questionnaires.

FACTORS INVESTIGATED

Both the small-firm owner-managers and the loan officers of the financial institutions were sent questionnaires which probed the following themes:

- Major threats to the survival of Small Firms
- Working capital sources and problems
- Fixed asset finance sources and problems
- Borrowing frequency
- Adequacy of sources of finance
- Expertise and major activities of the owner-manager
- Personnel problems

- Marketing problems
- Impact of the legal framework in which the business operates
- Knowledge of foreign economic environments (including government aid)
- General management problems

In addition, SME owner-managers were asked about the specialist staff they employed, what they spent on training, and what education they themselves had received. They were also asked for certain factual data on the size and origins of their businesses, and their attitudes to growth were probed.

FIs were asked also about their non-financial services, the criteria which they used for risk assessment, their risk premiums, security requirements and attitudes to non-commercial organisations.

Implicit in the research design was the assumption that SMEs are an important but declining sector of the economies of western industrial nations. Thus the broad objective was to assist policy formation towards small firms based on hard research rather than pressure from vociferous minority interests. As far as owner-managers of SMEs were concerned, it was intended to throw light on their strengths and weaknesses vis-a-vis their own company structures and their financial environment. With FIs, the intention was to probe their perceptions of, and attitudes towards, SMEs in general and the owner-managers of SMEs in particular.

RESULTS OF THE STUDY

Threats to the Survival of SMEs

When asked to rank the most important threats to the survival of their businesses, SME owner-managers in all three countries chose the same three reasons, although not in the same order:

West Germany:

1. Availability of finance
2. Marketing problems
3. Difficulty in complying with new laws and regulations

France:

1. Availability of finance
2. Difficulty in complying with new laws and regulations
3. Marketing problems

United Kingdom:

1. Difficulty in complying with new laws and regulations
2. Availability of finance
3. Marketing problems

Before discussing these results, it would be prudent to admit a shortcoming of this kind of broad-brush survey. When asked about general problem areas, naming the first two or three is easy; thereafter the choice and ordering may become contrived and arbitrary. For this reason we have only attached significance to the top three choices (which received far more endorsements than the others) rather than the list as a whole. Nevertheless, despite the different rank order in the three countries, the substantial similarity of perceptions is to be noted. The British preoccupation with legislative rather than financial problems is probably a consequence of the flood of health, safety, environmental and employment legislation to which small firms were subject in the seventies. Since this research dealt mainly with perceptions and attitudes rather than realities, it is quite possible that this mass of legislation may have appeared more burdensome than has actually proved to be the case in practice, especially in view of the rumour and suspicion engendered by much ill-informed comment at the time.(2) On the other hand, it is clear that similar problems beset the French and Germans (which may surprise British owner-managers who usually imagine that they have the worst environment to contend with). We return to this point below.

In complete contrast, FIs generally did not regard 'difficulty in complying with new laws and regulations' to be one of the major threats to the survival of SMEs. The exception was the French FIs, who rated it only third. This could be because the controllers in FIs do not themselves have to contend with most of the legislation referred to, or perhaps because they are better able to understand it in view of their (generally) more intensive training and education.

FIs in the three countries were also in substantial agreement among themselves as to the major threats faced by SMEs, viz.

West Germany:

1. Availability of finance
2. Management capability of owner
3. Marketing problems

France:

1. Management capability of owner
2. Availability of finance
3. Difficulty in complying with new laws and regulations

United Kingdom:

1. Availability of finance
2. Management capability of owner
3. Marketing problems

'Management capability of the owner' was not one of the choices on the SME questionnaire and at no stage were they asked to directly assess their own capabilities. While this omission makes the data not directly comparable, it is unlikely that candid or reliable answers would have been forthcoming. In any event, it was clearly of great importance to FIs, who consequently regarded the 'strength of management team' as one of their prime criteria for assessing risk in lending decisions.

It may therefore be inferred that 'availability of finance' substantially depends upon 'management capability of owner'. According to capital market theory finance will be available to all projects capable of earning more than the rate of interest; in practice, obtaining finance depends as much on the skill with which a proposal is presented, and the suitability of the FIs approached, as upon whether the proposition is actually viable. Subsequent answers to questions on risk criteria suggested that in France and Germany there is even more emphasis on 'backing the man', as well as on the use of mathematical assessment techniques, than in the UK.

Availability of Finance

Despite the confirmation by FIs of the owner managers' perception that 'Availability of Finance' was a major problem for SMEs, upon more detailed examination it did not appear obvious that this was the case in reality. The following results illustrate this:

SMEs

	UK	France	Germany
% having no problems raising finance	46	25	26
% having no problems in raising working capital	56	na	54.5
% having no problems in negotiating for funds for fixed assets	53	na	50
% who had had a confident request for finance unexpectedly rejected	13	27	6
% who felt existing financial institutions did not meet needs of smaller businesses	20	47	18.5

FIs

	UK	France	Germany
% who felt private sector finance met needs of smaller businesses for:			
Short term loans	87	89	79
Medium term loans	81	83	75
Long term loans	18.5	61	41.5
Property loans	18.5	39	37.5
Working capital	87	39	75
% who thought existing financial institutions did NOT meet needs of smaller businesses	4	4	na

It would appear that the more specific the question, the fewer SMEs or FIs admit to financing difficulties. Only the French seemed to indicate serious difficulties and that in raising working capital. Why this should be so is not totally clear, but it was partly confirmed when SMEs were questioned about the recent frequency of their borrowing; the French displayed rather more long than short-term borrowing, in contrast to the Germans and the British.

The results suggest that the ranking of 'Availability of finance' as a major threat to SME survival by their owner-managers is a kind of Pavlovian reaction, rather like farmers blaming the weather for all their difficulties. If this were not the case, it would be very hard to explain why a much higher level of specific financing problems was not identified by respondents. As far as FIs are concerned, it is natural for them to regard themselves as of crucial importance to their customers' survival, but they may be over-rating themselves or thinking too much in terms of those SMEs whom they have to help rather than the large proportion who evidently have little or no experience of borrowing from them.

Sources of Finance and Borrowing Habits

That personal and family wealth, retained earnings and banks of one kind or another were the main sources of finance for SMEs in each country was not a surprising result. Nor was it that FIs awarded themselves primacy of importance and minimised the role of other sources. Points of note included the popularity among SMEs of Hire Purchase and Leasing in Britain and France, but not in Germany and the relative unimportance of venture and development capital organisations in all three countries. Few SMEs resorted to Merchant Banks, but when they did do so this source was regarded as very important indeed.

Borrowing patterns among each national sample are best described as erratic. In no country did the overall incidence of borrowing appear high, (although it was highest in Germany but lowest in Britain). The Germans and French evinced very disciplined borrowing habits; that is, they claimed they borrowed long-term for good long-term reasons like relocation, diversification, expansion and re-equipment. There was little evidence of crisis borrowing (short-term borrowing to pay immediate operating expenses) but the British were inclined to borrow short for modernising equipment. The British SMEs also showed very little interest in borrowing for research and development purposes, in contrast to the Germans and, particularly, the French. Borrowing short thus seems a symptom of a general reluctance to make forward plans and commitments, a tendency that the UK overdraft system may well encourage.

Both FIs and SMEs were questioned at length about the limiting factors in lending decisions for both working capital and fixed assets. The major difference between countries was apparent here. Large majorities in Britain and Germany indicated government policy directives were scarcely considered (their SMEs confirming this opinion), whereas in contrast a majority of French SMEs thought government directives the most important factor in FIs lending decisions. This tendency is likely to increase since the election of a Socialist government in France.

It was also clear that communication between SMEs and FIs over the real reasons for refusal to make advances was lacking. Tiny proportions of SMEs (none in the UK sample) indicated that 'reservations regarding management team' had been quoted to them as a factor in negating a lending decision. In view of previous FI reservations upon owner-managers' capabilities, it is evident someone is not being frank.

Either FIs rarely express their opinions of SME owner-managers to them, or the latter decline to admit it. Whatever the cause it seems likely that there is a major role for management education to play in increasing the efficiency of this interface.

Expertise, Effort and Education

Owner-managers in each country claimed most expertise in the areas of production, finance and marketing. The Germans claimed the most expertise overall. They also claimed to expend most effort in these three areas, as did the British, but the French did not claim to use their talents with such apparent efficiency, expending effort on marketing and research and development far in excess of the expertise they claimed. However, all three sets of FIs agreed among themselves but totally disagreed with SMEs on this issue! Production was the only area in which FIs though SMEs possessed notable expertise. However, their efforts were seen as widely and inconsistently diffused, with marketing pre-occupying the French and Germans and finance the British and Germans. Substantially greater overall expertise, and quite Herculean efforts, were attributed to German SME owner-managers by their FIs. Whether or not the expertise and effort attributed is real or not, this perception alone is likely to make the SME/FI relationship in the Federal Republic a much more productive one.

In fact, the limited evidence suggests that no greater confidence is warranted in Germany than in the UK. In general the reservations expressed about owner-manager capability seem well-founded. Although the German owner-managers ceased full time education significantly later than their British or French counterparts, only 25% had had any specialist management training, (the same proportion as the British). Nor did the Germans or British compensate for their lack of training by employing large numbers of specialist managers. 45% of the British SMEs employed no professionally qualified staff at all, with production, marketing and finance again the favoured areas for those who did employ such staff. The Germans presented a similar picture. The French employed far more such specialised staff, only 17% employing none and 71% employing professionally qualified production staff. Moreover, the French complained of a shortage of suitably qualified specialists as a serious staff problem, which the British and Germans did not. This suggests that the more of these people the French employ, the more they appreciate them and the more they want. Perhaps this is a pointer for other countries.

Specific Problem Areas

Replies to these questions were interesting insofar as (1) in aggregate, they suggested a very moderate level of specific, identifiable problems experienced by the SMEs of all three countries, and (2) a not much higher level as diagnosed by their FIs.

The major exception was in the marketing area. Difficulty in passing on cost increases in prices and difficulty in competing with large firms on price were cited as the main problems. In each country SMEs appeared to operate in reasonably competitive markets (judging by the numbers who complained of domination of their markets by large firms), despite the sample structure. This means the extent to which SMEs in general feel their market is dominated by large firms was certainly understated in this survey and is an area which calls for substantial further research.

Economic Environments

Without exception, all groups in all countries perceived the other countries' economic environments as superior for SMEs compared to their own. (The American environment was also included as a choice category.) This extensive disagreement meant that no country stood out as clearly perceived to have a superior environment. The only area of agreement was that the UK had the worst economic environment - all but one group (French FIs) thought this. They rated it third so that they could rate their own environment 4th (and worst).

It is very doubtful if many of the views expressed were based on direct experience; more likely they were the consequence of rumour and a little knowledge, together with an ample element of 'the grass is always greener' syndrome. Few among all the groups could give examples of advantages possessed by foreign environments, and of those who did, most were vague and inaccurate. However, the external widespread grassroots perception of the economic environment in Britain is very disturbing and cannot but adversely effect the prospects of small British exporters.

Origin

The great majority of SMEs in all three countries had been started by the present owner (with or without a partner) or a member of the owner's family. Only the French sample was composed as much of entrepreneurs as inheritors: the majority of British and German owners had gone into existing family businesses. This predominance of family businesses partly explains and supports FIs concern over owners' management capabilities, since many owed their positions to ownership and inheritance rather than training, track-record and merit.

Growth

Majorities of SME owner managers in all three countries expressed a desire for growth, either in a new product or their existing line. Surprisingly perhaps, the British appeared rather more growth-oriented than the Germans. However it is easy to express a wish on paper, less so to put it into practice. German growth records speak for themselves. The relative lack of inclination to grow among the French can be partly explained by employment legislation that affects firms with more than 49 employees. This danger of creating artificial barriers to growth by imposing legislative size-bands is one which needs to be constantly born in mind in other countries, including the UK.

SUMMARY

There are five main conclusions from this research:

(a) Small manufacturing enterprise owner-managers in all three countries share similar perceptions of most problems. The French, however, have more difficulty raising working capital, employ more professionally qualified staff but are less inclined towards growth.

(b) Financial institution managers of all three countries have similar views of SMEs and their problems.

(c) There are many areas of agreement and shared perception between SMEs and FIs but:

  (i) FIs have grave reservations over the management capabilities of the owner managers with whom they deal.

  (ii) FIs regard production as the only area in which SME owner-managers possess substantial expertise.

  (iii) FIs rate their own importance to SMEs as higher than SMEs perceive it.

  (iv) FIs tend to take a rather more severe view of the problems SMEs face.

(d) All groups think some other country's economic environment for SMEs better than their own, but nearly all regard the UK environment as worst.

(e) The availability of finance is widely regarded as a major difficulty facing SMEs but the evidence to support this is difficult to identify in any of the countries studied, at least within the limits of this sampling frame.

REFERENCES

(1) D S Watkins. Final Report on SSRC Project HR 4543, 1981. Available from the New Enterprise Centre, Manchester Business School.

(2) Compare the paper by Westrip in this volume.

ACKNOWLEDGEMENT

The French and German data on which this paper in part draw were collected and collated by Professor W Straver of INSEAD and Professor E Paussenberger of the University of Giessen respectively.

8 Small firms policy in Baden-Wurttenberg: some UK implications

ALLAN GIBB
Durham University Business School

INTRODUCTION

This paper is based on a short in-depth study of the institutional framework for small firms development in Baden Wurttemberg in the Federal Republic of Germany. The underlying objective of the study was to provide a stimulus in terms of new, but tried, ideas for improved provision for small and medium-sized firms in the UK. There are always considerable barriers to the 'transfer of technology' of this sort from one country to another and it is frequently argued that 'cultural' and basic organisational differences provide the major barrier to this. The truth of this is self-evident: to stop there, however, underestimates the potential of policies to structure cultural response in the longer run and adapt and shape organisations in the short run. This paper endeavours to take this point into account by making a distinction between: the underlying political philosophy; the organisational structure and the way this is used; and the specific policy actions. In discussion of specific policy measures, what is taken as important is the degree of success of the measures, how they work in practice and the criteria that might be used for evaluating action in this respect in the UK. The implications follow naturally from this. In weighting implications for UK policy it is, however, important to underline that 'cause and effect' deductions cannot be made. Thus, for example, if the amount of small firms assistance is substantially greater in West Germany than in the UK, it cannot be inferred that the apparently more substantial small firm sector is a result of this. It may indeed be a cause! This point will be returned to in the conclusion.

Baden Wurttemburg was chosen as an area for study not only because of its long track record of specialist assistance for the small firm. Although the region has no natural resources it has: the highest income per head in Western Germany; the strongest manufacturing base; the highest proportion of small firms within that base, accounting for between 40 and 50% of output; a history of substantial and rapid growth; low unemployment; and a very high export capability(1).

The industrial base of the region is concentrated on capital goods production, which accounts for 50% of all industrial sales and almost 75% of industrial exports. Three industries, mechanical engineering, electrical engineering, and vehicles employ 45% of all industrial workers. The performance of certain of these sectors in economic growth has been outstanding. Over the past 20 years the electrical engineering industry has increased its real turnover by 8 times and the mechanical engineering and vehicles industries by 5 times. One of the major factors behind this development has been the growth in exports(2). Almost one-quarter of capital goods industry output is now exported, double the proportion of 20 years ago.

Estimated gross national product of Baden Wurttemberg was DM202m in 1978. This has increased fourfold in real terms since 1972. Income per head was estimated at DM18,476: it is estimated to be the highest of any state in West Germany(3).

The economy of Baden Wurttemberg demonstrates that it is possible to have a very prosperous manufacturing and export orientated economy based on a very substantial small firms contribution.

Baden Wurttemberg is one of the 10 states of the Federal Republic of West Germany, with a population of just over 9m. It has its own Parliament, Cabinet of Ministers (with a Prime Minister) and enjoys a great deal of autonomy in its financial, economic and education policies as well as in jurisdiction, internal administration, etc. Its location in South West Germany gives it easy access to Switzerland, France, Italy and Austria. Stuttgart is the administrative centre.

THE PHILOSOPHY OF SMALL FIRMS POLICY

Small firms policy has a deeper (and longer standing) philosophical base in West Germany than in the UK. In economic terms it is seen clearly as an arm of competition policy: in social terms it is seen as the centrepiece of a commitment to bolster certain middle class entrepreneurial and cultural values as a barrier to polarisation between corporate management and unions. These two aims of policy provide the strong 'structuralist' case for subsidisation of the small firms sector. The employment criteria much publicised in the UK as a basis for small firm support forms only one minor part of these arguments. The controversial point debated extensively by Bolton (and subsequently on many occasions since) concerning the distorting effects of subsidising the small firms sector is assumed away under the argument that the sector is 'disadvantaged' in terms of a number of criteria including market entry, access to capital and technology information and advice, training and counselling. In applying these criteria very little distinction is made between manufacturing and service industry. This opens the way for a considerable aid programme which nevertheless sets out clearly to avoid 'propping up' operations, insists on counterpart 'self help' to go with official funds and seeks to operate through existing institutions rather than directly through government. In these principles both Federal and State Government seem to be at one, with the latter operating under a comprehensive law setting out clearly the extensive nature of the provisions and their basis(4).

The principles are set out clearly in Federal and Land publications. Current Federal policy stems from the Bundestag paper 7/5248(5) of 21st May 1979 'Report of the Federal Government on Small Firms Policy', the main elements of which are incorporated in a brief guide 'Small Business - efficiency and competition' published in August 1978(6). Land policy stems from the spcial 'Law to Promote Small and Medium Sized Firms' of 16th December 1975(7). These dates, however, obscure the fact that small firms policies are not new in Germany. Indeed, they have been a prominent part of post-war German economic philosophy as evolved by Professor L Erhard, Minister of Economies in successive post-war German governments. They have their root in Erhard's policies to prevent the revival of old class differences arising out of income disparity which had contributed to the rise of Hitler. Support of small and medium businesses was an important strand of this policy(8). The Baden Wurttemberg Land, however, claims that its planned state promotion of small enterprise pre-dates Erhard by some years (going back to 1848)(9).

The kernel of West Germany's small firms promotional philosophy lies in the concept of a 'balanced economy'. The promotion of small firms plays a major role in this by providing balance in competition, a balance in job opportunity and a social balance in society through the preservation of 'mittellstand' ('middle class' or 'self employed') values(10). The first purportedly prevents the exploitation of monopoly power(11): the latter two help prevent the polarisation of conflict between corporate big business and unions(12). These balances are complemented by the contribution of small firms to 'structuring the economy at the regional and local level' (ie. to regional balance) and the availability of local job opportunities within easy travel to work patterns. All these points are clearly spelt out in the literature(13).

Both Federal and Land Governments are in agreement about the specific aims of policy. These are(14):

- the viability and competitiveness of small and medium sized firms in industrial society
- an increase in the efficiency of small business
- successful adjustment of small firms to structural changes

Underlying these aims, however, is the important assumption that small firms are disadvantaged as noted above. This is a fundamental tenet of both Federal and State legislation, and is clearly stated as such. It is this that opens the door for a wide variety of discriminatory policies leading to special subsidies for(15):

- vocational and management training
- consultancy and finance
- special emphasis on start-ups, technical development and innovation, co-operation, purchasing and exporting

It is worth noting that by and large these policies not only do not discriminate between the service and manufacturing sector, but even extend to the professions.

Notwithstanding the clear commitment to subsidy the operating principles under both Federal and State legislation are(16):

> 'That policies should not serve to preserve outdated structures.'
>
> 'That they should be geared to strengthen the ability of the small firm to help itself.'
>
> and
>
> 'That (as far as possible) existing organisations and self-help institutions are responsible for these measures ...'(17)

Thus action must be forward looking, be matched by resources from the small firm itself and, wherever possible, should be undertaken by non-government institutions.

Some Contrasts with the UK

Clearly there are some major contrasts with the UK. Perhaps the most obvious is the lack of a clear statement of small firms policy as such with its underlying assumptions. Post-Bolton it can be argued that UK small firms policy has been marginalist, based on the identification of individual areas of specific disadvantage of the small firm in the marketplace. As Bannock has pointed out(18), however, it must be recognised that the present 'market' economic structure is heavily distorted and, as such, decisions taken by institutions and companies on 'commercial grounds' reflect their own commercial advantage but not necessarily consumer preferences. Moreover, small firms policy has not been seen at all as an area of competition policy, it being assumed that anti-monopoly legislation will be an adequate means of defending market entry. There is also no sign of a policy having a 'social' aspect other than perhaps as a means of providing job opportunities. Indeed, policy debate recently, helped by academic research, is being led along this narrow line(19). Such parsimony may also be responsible for the UK policy of limiting certain types of assistance largely to the manufacturing sector. Finally, it is clear that the regionalisation of decision-making, natural in a Federal state, is in major contrast with UK centralisation which makes it difficult for the small firm with its local orientation to articulate its needs and contribute pressure for change.

THE REGIONAL, INSTITUTIONAL FRAMEWORK FOR SMALL FIRMS POLICY

The philosophy of both the Federal Government nationally and the Land Government in Baden Wurttemberg is to channel policies as far as possible through existing organisations(20). A distinction can be made between the 'software' (advice, information, counselling and training) and 'hardware' (finance and resource provision) policies. The former are channelled mainly through the existing membership organisations of businesses; the latter through specialist state organisations but linked with the private sector. The Chambers of Commerce (Handelskammers), the Chambers of Handicraft (Handwerkskammers), the Productivity Association (Nationaliserungs - Kuratorium der Deutschen Wirtschaft - RDW) and the Industry and Trade Associations are the main providers of 'software'. The universities and technical colleges play a very limited direct role in provision, although they do play a major role in a scheme designed to encourage the use of college staff in technical consultancy in small firms. The universities also provide staff for some small firm training programmes. There are also a number of specialist institutes for research, innovation and management training largely independent of the universities. On the 'hardware' side, State specialised finance is channelled through the State Landeskreditbank (but usually in co-operation with the private banks) and is backed by the loan guarantee bank, the Burgschaftsbank, which has both private and state involvement.

Land support for both hardware and software is almost wholly channelled through the Office of Trade and Industry (Landesgewerbeamt). This office is responsible for the implementation of industrial policy and is virtually wholly concerned with assistance to small and medium sized firms. It has a staff of several hundred employees. Its services include: information provision, the development and subsidising of courses for management; advice on factory planning and location; operation and funding of counselling and consultancy schemes; design, technology transfer and innovation; licensing, patenting and organisation of exhibitions. Effectively it is the funding source for most of the assistance given to small firms in the region, acting as a vehicle for both Land and Federal funds.

There is no Federal Office at the Land level. Federal funding for software is therefore either channelled through the Landesgewerbeamt or directly to the associations through their national organisations. Whereas the Federal Government is in partnership with the Land on software, it tends to operate its own parallel policies in provision of finance. Its main involvement is through the European Recovery Programme (ERP) funds (see below) which are largely channelled through national banks.

Most of the official funding goes through the Handelskammers (Chambers of Commerce) and Handwerkskammers (Chambers of Handicrafts). There are 12 Chambers of Industry and Commerce in Baden Wurttemberg. With the exception of craftsmen, who must be members of the Handwerkskammers (see below) all individuals or firms engaged in trade and industry must be members of the local Chamber and must pay a levy which varies with profits. An average fee for small and medium firms might be DM100 a year.

There are 7 Handwerkskammers in Baden Wurttemberg. They represent some 96,000 small businesses in 125 occupations. These occupations are not, however, necessarily traditional craft industries but may include various types of engineering and electrical activities.

In addition to the Handwerkskammers in Baden Wurttemberg, there are gilds for various professions. In Stuttgart, for example, there are between 40 and 50 of these. Membership is not compulsory. Each of these gilds is assembled into a loose kreishandwerkskschaft. There are 7 kreishandwerkschafts in the greater Stuttgart area. As not all the members of the Handwerkskammer are in gilds, the kreishandwerkschafts do not represent all local firms. Indeed, they do not have individual members: only the gilds themselves are members.

There are, however, also associations of gilds (fachverbands) at the regional level which might relate to one or several professions. For example, the Metallfachverband Baden Wurttemberg is an association of five metal crafts representing 50 gilds in the region. The verband is voluntary, as are the gilds, and therefore its membership will not necessarily consist of all members of the trade.

Finally, there are the trade associations for most branches and groups of trade and industry outside of handwerks. Unlike the LHKs and HKs, membership is voluntary. They may provide training, counselling and advice to member firms and may be concerned with setting standards for skills training in member companies. Industry trade associations also provide a vehicle for implementation of Federal and Land schemes.

The membership associations are complemented by the RKW, the national productivity association, which has 11 regional centres, one of which is in Stuttgart. Membership is voluntary and includes companies, unions and both private and public sector organisations. The RKW provides information on production and operates consultancy and training schemes. In Baden Wurttemberg the RKW has 1900 members, most of whom are small and medium sized companies. It receives support from both Land and Federal Government.

The education sector plays no major specific institutional part in small firm policies other than through a special foundation, the Steinbeis Stiftung. This provides the umbrella organisation in Baden Wurttemberg for the operation of a technical consultancy service (Die Aufgaben der Technischen Beratungsidienste) (TBD). The aim is to link effectively the skills and knowledge of staff in the Engineering Colleges in the region with the needs of small firms. The scheme operates with 14 colleges throughout the region and is directed from Aalen. The foundation is supported by private companies and by State funds.

Of other specialist institutes in the region, two deserve special mention. The Institut fur Technik der Betriebsfuhrung im Handwork (ITB) (Institute for Management Techniques in Handicraft) is one of 7 special national institutions associated with the German Handicrafts Institute and the only one located in Baden Wurttemberg. It is also the only one of the 7 that has specialist responsibility for management. As such it serves the whole of the Federal Republic. It is funded mainly by the Federal Government and Lander (collectively). The development and implementation of management training programmes, together with research into the management of handicraft firms, are its two major responsibilities. The Fraunhofer Gessellschaft is part of a private society which, however, is funded by both Federal and State Government. There are 22 institutions throughout the Federal Republic of which 8 are located in Baden Wurttemberg. The Institute is a society for the advancement of applied research and aims at providing a bridge with industry through contract research. Only a small part of its work is, however, concerned with small and medium firms.

At the regional level there are two specialist financial institutions supported by the Land who work closely with the private sector. Federal aid is either channelled through the Land or through private banks by national specialist institutions. The Landeskreditbank (State credit bank) is owned 100% by the Land and is effectively the arm of the Land concerned with the financial aspects of small firms policy. Since 1973 it has been dealing exclusively in subsidised loans provision to small firms, usually by means of subsidised interest rates. It has a large number of specialist programmes. The Burgschaftsbank (Guarantee bank) is a specialist bank operating loan guarantees for private sector lending. This bank grew out of the Credit Guarantee Associations operated by the various industry associations. The bank also operates a subsidiary (Mittelstandische Beteilligungsgesellschaft) which provides equity participation in small firms.

Some Contrasts with the UK

The obvious contrast with the UK is the concentration in the channelling of funds and policies through the membership organisations of the small firms. This, of course, is facilitated by the strength of the membership organisations themselves, reinforced by statute. Such a structure facilitates 'ownership' of small firm activities by the firms themselves which can be the key to successful implementation of many policies. While there are presently those who advocate a move towards giving the UK Chambers(21) similar powers, there are probably substantial barriers to this. Notwithstanding the institutional debate, the principle of co-ordination of small firm activities at the regional level seems important, given the local orientation of most small firms. This is not synonymous with the creation of an all-purpose bureaucracy but can effectively be channelled through appropriate and different local institutions for different purposes. Where these do not exist the creation of local foundations may be appropriate for specific purposes. The UK has yet to produce a regional institutional framework.

THE BROAD CATEGORIES OF SPECIAL ASSISTANCE TO SMALL FIRMS

In line with Federal and Land Government philosophy, the small and medium business in Baden Wurttemberg is eligible for a variety of subsidised assistance, both 'software' (advice, training, consulting) and 'hardware' (finance and research). On the 'software' side these are seen as providing a stimulus for the small firm to broaden its view of the environment, encourage its acceptability of modern techniques and develop professional management. The underlying rationale for specialist assistance on the 'hardware' side is that there is a situation of chronic deficiency of personal capital which threatens the growth and development of new and existing businesses(22).

The key software areas are as follows:

Management Training

Both the Federal and Land Governments of Baden Wurttemberg have made substantial commitments to entrepreneurial training. The Federal Government in its policy statements describes measures for 'advanced training of entrepreneurs and their staff'(23). These embrace support for courses and institutions involved in training entrepreneurs, development of trainers and consultants and provision of relevant literature. The Land in its special law governing the development of small and medium sized firms indicates that it will grant allowances for 'recognised' courses and programmes as well as for technical training.

Entrepreneurial training can broadly be categorised into:

(i) Appreciation programmes: aimed at giving an overview of the management of an owner-managed firm to a population of potential entrepreneurs, eg. apprentices or those studying for 'masters' certificates.

(ii) Start your own business programmes: aimed specifically at those with a declared intention to start their own company.

(iii) Small business management programmes: aimed at all aspects (including technical) of managing a small company.

Although the basic provision is there for support of all types of small firms programmes, in practice subsidies for courses are given very discriminately and are concentrated mainly on category (ii) above.

In Baden Wurttemberg, however, it is possible, for example, for the small and medium sized company to obtain a fairly clear guide to programmes throughout the region and in its particular locality by means of the local Chambers of Commerce and Handicrafts. It is these organisations and not the education sector which provide the administration for programmes. The RKW is the major vehicle through which the Chamber of Commerce programmes are organised: it offers over 300 courses a year throughout the region, most of which are appropriate for the small company. The Handwerkskammers provide their own specialist programmes. The education sector contributes staff for some of these programmes but many are manned by specialists from consulting organisations.

Training programmes for start-ups are heavily subsidised: also subsidised are several courses aimed at providing specialist training for very small firm owners and managers, together with an industry 'problem centred' training approach sponsored by the Federal Government.

Counselling Support

The support for consultancy is seen by both Federal and State Governments to be part of 'structural' policy aimed at increasing the efficiency and competitiveness of small firms. The prime aim seems to be to 'open up' the small firm to the environment and to educate it in the use of consultant services. The subsidised programmes were therefore seen as a form of 'pump priming'.

The emphasis in Baden Wurttemberg is on providing consultancy either through subsidy of the open market or direct employment of professional consultants. The service is funded both by Federal and Land Governments in varying proportions, but is not undertaken directly by either. It is channelled through the Handelskammers, the Handwerkshammers, the RKW and the Trade Associations. The 'basic' scheme is for the provision of a minimum free consultancy (usually of up to 2 days a year) with a further period of subsidised consultancy (usually up to 15 days in any 5 years). This is open to virtually all small firms in Baden Wurttemberg (including a number of the professions). It is complemented by a number of special schemes including one for start-ups. Consultant staffing policy varies: certain of the institutions employ their own consultants while also putting out work to the 'free market'. There are, however, controls on the selection of external consultants; and internal staff consultants have to undertake substantial training programmes. Total spending on the consultants programme was approximately DM3.5m in 1979 in Baden Wurttemberg(24).

The Landesgewerbeamt had no detailed evaluation of the workings of the consultancy schemes, although currently research is being undertaken at national level into the need for consulting by small and medium sized businesses.

Hardware

Special Financial Assistance Measures

Finance for the small firm must be seen in the context of the difference in the banking system between Germany and the UK. The main differences(25) are:

(i) The typical German bank is a 'universal' bank providing a full range of commercial and investment banking services. The traditional separation as in the UK of commercial and investment or merchant banks and the complete separation of stockbrokers does not exist. Thus while there is a wide variety of institutions (see below) in terms of legal form, business structure, organisation, size and fields of business activity, no fundamental separation of functions exist.

(ii) As a result, private commercial banks in particular very often hold substantial interests in commercial and other businesses.

(iii) A very large part of the banking system is regionalised or localised:

(a) Of the 280 private commercial banks 113 are regional banks*.

*Which may, however, cover more than one region.

(b) These are complemented by local savings banks. These banks are not incorporated under private law but are municipal and district institutions incorporated under public law usually pursuant to State (Land) statutes. Contrary to what the name implies they offer the same all-round service as commercial banks. In 1976 there were 649 savings banks in the Federal Republic with assets of DM620b. These are the largest group of banking institutions in Germany.

(c) The co-operative banking system is also important and has grown out of the local credit associations. These were originally only intended to provide services for members but now tend to offer their services to non-members. They also conduct their business as 'universal' banks but with emphasis on short and medium term lending business. There are over 2400 Credit Associations in Germany.

(iv) Out of co-operation between the regional and local banks and Chambers of Commerce and Handicrafts in Germany, a system of Credit Guarantee emerged after the Second World War, often associated with specific industries such as furniture, metalworking, etc. These institutions have facilitated the Federal and Land Governments support of loan guarantee schemes (see below).

(v) A certain pecularity arises in the banking system because of the use of Marshall Aid Funds associated with post-Second World War Recovery Programmes. Part of the European Recovery Aid was set aside for small and medium sized businesses in line with the Erhard economic philosophy. The European Recovery Programme(26) budget for small business was DM975m in 1978, much of which was channelled through specialist banks, ie. the Lastenausgletchsbank in Bonn and the Kreditanstalt fur Weideraufbau in Frankfurt.

The implications of these differences for the attitude to lending to small and medium firms are fairly obvious and include:

(a) An industrial orientation of the banking system.

(b) A strong local orientation of the banking system. It is the local co-operative, savings and peoples' banks that undertake the bulk of small firms business. Indeed, the survival of these banks is directly associated with the health of local industry which they obviously have a vested interest in fostering. Their close links with the Chambers, their origins in some cases in particularly industries, their close dependence on, and knowledge of, local markets and their desire to keep funds and business in the region are all important motivating factors in their courtship of the small firm(27).

(c) The association of the Credit Associations and banks with local credit guarantee schemes has also had an impact on their attitudes to take extra business through these programmes(28).

(d) The fundamental post-war philosophy underlying the ERP special programms for small and medium businesses was based on recognition of the low personal capital base of those seeking to start businesses. This has conditioned the approach, not only to the gearing of lending (see below), but also to the need to subsidise it in a variety of ways, particularly for the new businessman. The 'tradition' of special support for lending to business starters is therefore not new to Germany.

Key Areas of Support by Land Institutions

In Baden Wurttemberg the Land has its own specialist credit institution (the Landeskreditbank). This is wholly owned by the Land and directly supervised by the Finance Ministry of Baden Wurttemberg. It operates a number of specialist programmes for small firm financing. The basic service offered is that of subsidised interest rates for loans covering periods of 10 to 20 years with facility for delaying capital repayments. The programmes include.

1. Support for start-ups and acquisition of small firms in industry, handicrafts, services and professions

2. Assistance with relocation of small firms

3. Assistance with rationalisation of product or process

4. Assistance to firms moving to economically weak (assisted) regions

5. Special tourist investment programmes

6. Special programmes for war veterans and refugees

7. Special programmes to assist firms with liquidity problems

8. Special programmes to assist with innovations in small firms

The LKB funds obtained from the Land are used to subsidise the cost of its own borrowing from the market, enabling it to relend at low interest rates. The incentive for the private banks to refer clients is that they can then back small investment schemes jointly while obtaining some additional revenue from this activity. With interest rates (at the time of the visit - January/February 1980) at around 9-10%, the interest subsidy of up to 5% was obviously significant. By far the most important loan programme is that relating to start-ups with 3800 loans granted in 1979 out of 4500 applications. In 1973 successful loan applications numbered 270.

Part of the special lending programme of the LKB is tied in with specialist regional assistance. Despite the low average level of unemployment (less than 3% compared with between 5-6% for West Germany as a whole), the region has a comprehensive programme of assistance for special areas. Within the Land there are 3 priority areas, 4 development areas, and 11 development centres (community based). The incentives range up to a maximum of assistance of 20% of the total investment. In the designation of special areas, criteria of both the Federal and Land Governments is used.

In practice the Land has sought to complement Federal assistance (supported by the EEC) for improvement of regional structure, with its own areas of economic weakness or structural imbalance. For example, the watch-making industry in the central area of Baden Wurttemberg has been badly hit by cheaper imports and is being assisted in the restructuring process. Generally, however, the criteria for a designated area is that of unemployment, with the areas attracting maximum assistance having over 4-5% unemployed.

A system of loan guarantees has been operating in Baden Wurttemberg since the 1950s. Credit guarantee associations for all important sectors of 'mittelstand' business were established covering:

Crafts
Wholesale and retail business
Hotel and catering trade
Horticulture
Transport and distribution
Medium and small industry

Members of these associations are the representative organisations of the sector, ie. trade and industry associations, chambers of industry and commerce, and industrial companies (including large-scale enterprises). The system was originally managed by 4 umbrella Credit

Guarantee Associations owned by the Chambers and Industrial Associations with private bank participation. These Associations are now (in Baden Wurttemberg) amalgamated into the Burgschaftsbank in which the 4 major partners are the Associations. The loan guarantee system is available throughout Germany but the institutional arrangements vary. The guarantee funds have (in the 1970s) been added to by the Federal Government through the ERP as well as by the Land.

The loan guarantee system offers to the private bank and the customer the opportunity to extend the loan to amounts which could not be satisfactorily secured. The Burgschaftsbank will normally guarantee 80% of the outstanding amount. Thus, for example, in the case of a loan request for DM100,000, of which DM50,000 could be secured in the normal way, then the Burgschaftsbank may give a guarantee of up to 80% of the DM50,000 at risk. In the early days the bank would cover all of the risk but this has been found to be unnecessary because of the low loss rates and the private banks have been encouraged to share some of the risk (the loss rate is less than one per cent on total guaranteed loans to date: as a per cent of all guaranteed loans that have been repaid to date it is less than 3%).

The activities of the Burgschaftsbank are underwritten by the Land and the Federal Government, who jointly give counter-guarantees for the loans guaranteed by the bank. Three-fifths of the support is provided by the Federal Government and the remainder by the Land. The level of this counter-guarantee was originally 80% of the guaranteed amount but has since fallen to 60%, largely because of the good track record of the bank(29). In addition, however, ERP funding can be used to meet (write off) up to twelve-and-a-half per cent of any default, in addition to the normal back-up guarantees given by the Land and Federal Governments. The Land is represented on the 'guarantee committee' through which all applications have to proceed, and by this means also represents the Federal Government.

To complement the activity of the Burgschaftsbank in cases where loan guarantees are insufficient to facilitate adequate capital provision, a separate equity company, 'Mittelstandische Beteiligungsgesellschaft', has been set up, offering equity participation to medium sized businesses.

Key Areas of Support by Federal Institutions

The Federal Government has involvement in loan guarantees by some of its support for the Burgschaftsbank. It also provides a variety of specialist assistance, complementing and competing with the activities of the Landeskreditbank, through its European Recovery Fund Programmes. In addition, it supports a specialist institution aimed at providing equity finance for small firms on special terms.

Following the completion of the post-war reconstruction programme, the provision of investment loans to improve the performance of small and medium sized businesses has been the main target for promotion by the ERP Special Fund.The major ERPs(30) for small business are as follows:

(i) Programmes to promote the establishment of enterprises

(ii) The ERP regional programme, financing for which has been described under 'Special Areas Assistance' above

(iii) Programmes to assist location induced expenditures

(iv) Programmes to promote the participation of private equity investment companies in small business

(v) Programmes of the Reconstruction Loan Corporation and the Equalisation of Burdens Bank, designed to provide long-term loans, channelled through the private banks

Special Measures to Assist with Premises

The issue of premises for small firms has been very important in the UK in recent years. Public programmes of small factories building, the operation of reduced rentals and rent-free periods and development of small workshop facilities have all become popular. In contrast, there was little official indication that premises for small firms were regarded as a problem in Baden Wurttemberg. Official assistance was therefore largely restricted to signposting and advice by the Chambers and Landesgewerbeamt.

The Landesgewerbeamt deals with the top end of the market: its special department for advice on locations had only 10 enquiries for facilities under 500 square metres in 1979. The office is in the process, however, of developing a comprehensive region-wide directly of facilities based on a computerised data bank with information from each Kreis (district).

Apart from the above offices, information on premises is left to private estate companies and property brokers. There are no state building corporations, few government factories or special provision by the public sector for small firms. There is some general subsidy, however, in urban areas for the provision of basic services to industrial sites.

The main provision in urban areas will be for the local authority to buy land, put in basic services and sell the plots to interested firms. The framework for industrial premises provision is provided by land-use plans which distinguish between mixed zones (of housing and usually small business), industrial zones and housing zones (with little business).

Some Contrasts with the UK

Training provision in the UK is already well developed through the programmes of the Training Services Division and Training Boards. In contrast to Germany, however, there is a gap in provision for the very small firm (under 20 employees). There is an area of extensive provision in Germany through the Hankwerkskammers and Association programmes. The Training Boards provide 'cut-off' points at around this level, and apart from limited ventures by Cosira and certain associations, there is little provision. This sector is possibly the seedbed for small firm development, yet is not cultivated. The cultivation of this seedbed may lie in building into basic apprenticeship education and further education programmes at all levels: the presentation of an image of possible self-employment; and certain of the necessary background skills to encourage entrepreneurship. It may also demand the extension of this principle back into the basic education system itself. There is also potential in the UK for the design and development of a basic programme aimed specifically at provision for the existing small businessman or young man working in a small business, perhaps with a diploma qualification. Such a qualification may assist in helping the businessman negotiate with institutions for resources, etc. The major contrast, however, lies in the absence of clear signposting at the regional level, the lack of collaboration between organisations undertaking this provision, and the absence of involvement of business associations.

The provision of subsidised consulting/counselling services to the small firm substantially exceeds that of the UK. Much greater use is made of the free market consultant. Linkages of the scheme with private sector organisations is much greater. Moreover, there is a differentiated pricing structure to give a larger amount of free assistance to the start-up and scale charges according to the size of the company. The service seems also to be more geared up than the UK counselling service to take a greater proportion of companies in the industrial, service and manufacturing sector in the size range 5-50 employees(31). It also offers specialised 'expert' services such as technical innovation, new product development, exporting, new investment and co-operation. However, as with the training services, it is linked through private sector organisations such as the Chambers of Commerce, Trade Associations, etc.

It is in the provision of finance that the basic philosophical commitment to small enterprise in West Germany is clearly underwritten in a manner which contrasts sharply with the UK. This commitment is made all the stronger by the equally contrasting universalist and regional structure of the German banking system. Perhaps most important is the regional orientation in provision of finance. It was stressed that it is the local commercial interdependence and close links of local banking and local business that provided the basis for sound understanding of financing needs. To simulate this in the UK would probably mean the creation of new institutions with local capital involvement. Without this it might be difficult to create the underlying philosophy prevalent in Baden Wurttemberg that capital availability is the biggest barrier to entry of new firms and that the start-up is capital deficient and needs to be assisted with generous attitudes to gearing. Moreover, a loan guarantee scheme might produce very little change without combination with some regional financial initiative. The local 'ownership' of the development of loan guarantees in Germany seems important in its success. It seems unlikely that any UK commitment would be made to the small firm sector in terms of long-term low interest rate finance, evident at both Federal and local level in Germany, and available particularly for start-ups. However, the problem of provision of equity capital on a buy-back basis seems more likely to be sympathetically considered in the future given existing initiatives(32).

KEY AREAS FOR SMALL FIRM POLICY

Within the overall framework of 'software' and 'hardware' measures certain key areas of emphasis are apparent in Baden Wurttemberg. The most visible are those relating to start-ups, innovation, public purchasing, expanding and group co-operation. These are all areas which are provided for by public policy in the UK, although the difference in emphasis and the nature of assistance seem to be substantial. It is beyond the scope of this paper to do more than provide a brief summary with comment on UK contrasts.

Assistance for Start-ups

In Baden Wurttemberg there is a major commitment to the encouragement of new businesses in all sectors by the specialist provision of free consultancy, free training programmes and subsidised finance. These include:

(i) Six days free consulting a year for the first 5 years of operation

(ii) Plus up to 50 days at a subsidised rate over the first 5 years

(iii) Provision of free, full-time and part-time training courses for all types of start-up

(iv) Subsidised long-term loans from the Land credit bank and through the Federal European Recovery Fund for up to half the interest cost

(v) A loan guarantee scheme between one-third and one-half of whose provision is for start-ups

In the UK, provision for counselling of start-ups is mainly through the Department of Industry Counselling Service. This is supplemented by ad hoc arrangements in different areas throughout the country, ranging from Enterprise North in the North East the the Enterprise Agencies in various city areas and connurbations and local authority/education sector initiatives. The private consulting sector is not involved as an arm of public policy. In the field of training, however, there are now a number of well established programmes under the auspicies of the

Training Services Division of the Manpower Services Commission at 4 University Business Schools throughout the UK and 16 colleges spread widely throughout the country. In addition to these facilities, there is the specialist provision of the Scottish and Welsh Development Agencies. There is, however, no widespread specialist provision of training assistance during the first years of the venture, when businesses are particularly vulnerable. There are a growing number of special schemes introduced by the banking system, Enterprise Agencies, Local Authorities, Trusts, etc aimed especially at the new starter, but there is no standard subsidised finance, although there is now a loan guarantee scheme and schemes with equity buy back provision.

Assistance for Innovation, Research, New Product/Process Development

Baden Wurttemberg has a range of 'software' and 'hardware' provisions supported by Land and Federal Government to encourage innovation, research and development and new product/process development in small and medium firms. The definition of small and medium for this purpose covers a wider range than is normal. The strategy spelt out clearly in the literature is to build bridges between small firms and sources of assistance including the educational systems. Among major provisions are:

(i) Specialist free consultancy. Available on several different models, some of which are financed experimentally by the Federal Government. Usually up to 2 or 3 days a year for problem analysis and linking with possible sources of help. This can also include data bank researchers, assistance with applications for finance, company linkages and training seminars.

(ii) Subsidised consulting (up to 30 days) on a sliding scape up to 75% of the cost, for new product development.

(iii) The linking of small firms with engineering college staff through a technical consultancy scheme subsidised by a foundation supported by the Land and private enterprise.

(iv) The provision of a regional technological signposting service, including detailed contact guide, data bank terminal, literature abstract service, patent office and design centre.

(v) Special funding to independent research foundations to reduce costs of contract research to smaller firms.

(vi) Subsidy of up to 40% of staff costs of personnel engaged in R&D.

(vii) Subsidy of up to 30% of cost of sub-contracted research for new product/process development.

(viii) Special interest free loans up to 50% (70% in special cases) for new product/process developments new to Germany (2 separate Federal and Land schemes).

(ix) Low interest rate loans for introduction of new products and processes through the Land credit bank.

There are a number of schemes in the UK concerned with the financing of R&D and innovation. What is missing compared with Germany seems to be the specialist provision of links between sources of assistance/ideas and the firms themselves. In particular there is little provision for providing specialist 'linking' advice to small firms which involves some expert assistance in diagnosing the problem and need. Moreover, there is no specialist model of linking polytechnics/universities and engineering departments by similar means to that employed in the German system. In recognising these 'ideas' there should be understanding of the limited success that German schemes seem to have had in encouraging technology transfer from large companies and from universities to small business(33). The most successful principle appears to be to start from the small firm itself and find the means to assist with its problems. Moreover, there is some recognition that 'software' support schemes may have to go further in providing assistance with marketing on new products and processes, rather than concentrate solely on technical aspects.

At this point in time the various financial incentive schemes at present operating in Germany are being evaluated, and the results should prove interesting to UK observers.

Assistance for Small Firms to Obtain a Share of Public Purchasing

There is clear recognition by Federal and Land authorities of the need to encourage public purchasing from small and medium firms. In particular:

(i) There are clear official guidelines to encourage the break-up of public contracts to facilitate small firms tendering.

(ii) These also embody regulations to ensure that certain categories of small firms within a given per cent of the preferred tender price get the opportunity to tender again.

(iii) The Land provisions also include a clause designed to ensure adequate consideration of small firm tenders within a certain per cent of the lowest price with provision for small firms to be given preference when their tender is competitive, even if they cannot supply the whole quantity.

(iv) There is a special procurement office at the regional level, funded by the Land and Chambers of Commerce and handwerk which: acts as a signposting service to all small firms in the region for opportunities to tender for Federal and Land procurement contracts; provides advice to companies in tendering; provides advice to public authorities; alerts local companies capable of tendering.

(v) The office provides opportunities for tender to a large number of small firms in any year.

The German system of encouragement of small firm involvement in public sector procurement highlights the possibilities that exist in making clearer provision for the breaking-up of public contracts, central and local, to facilitate small firms applying. Moreover, it highlights the potential for providing a focal specialist 'signposting and assistance' source at the regional level in recognition that one major barrier to greater small firms participation might be awareness of opportunity.

Assistance for Small Firm Co-operation

Recognition of the case for encouragement of small firm grouping is embodied in Federal and anti-trust policy. In reinforcement of this, assistance is given at the regional level in the form of:

(i) Free and subsidised consultancy for co-operation ventures

(ii) Signposting and advice on partnership opportunities through the productivity associations and chambers

(iii) Guidance by groups of small sub-contractors in preparing joint tendering for public contracts

In the UK the Department of Industry has had its own scheme to encourage group co-operation which has attracted little attention and success. Moreover, there is no systematic means of encouraging joint venture or joint tendering activities among small firms. The German emphasis lies in providing regional support and guidance for incentive to co-operation and facilitating joint venturing and tendering at the regional level.

Assistance for Exporting

Special assistance for encouragement of small firm exporting in Baden Wurttemberg includes:

(i) Free and subsidised consulting in addition to the general provision

(ii) Export training programmes, run by the chambers

(iii) Special loan guarantee scheme for export production

(iv) Financial support scheme for market entry in the form of a 50% grant for market research

Generally, support matches that available in the UK, the main contrasts being in the degree to which assistance is co-ordinated through one centre, the Chambers of Commerce and Hankwerk and the operation of a specialist loan guarantee scheme for export production.

SOME OVERALL IMPLICATIONS FOR THE UK

This paper has finished at the end of the beginning of the research process, namely that part concerned with observation. Even so, for reasons of space, it has been possible to give only a limited view of the workings of the small firms assistance framework at the regional (or at least state) level in West Germany. Yet it is precisely this picture that is often of most interest to policy-makers. Policy is (hopefully) the art of the possible: research objectives might therefore start with drawing attention to the major parameters and the 'process' by which events happen as much as the 'why' and the evaluation of their outputs. For if it is possible to emulate the process without great cost or radical change, then it is perhaps worthwhile to explore the policy further and to view its impact.

Such is arguably the case with much of what can be learned from Baden Wurttemberg. Without substantial change it would, for example, be possible to widen the scope of the Department of Industry counselling service to give a larger amount of free assistance to the start-up, and perhaps also increase the number of free counsellings to make a stronger initial impact on the company. There is scope, moreover, to broaden the coverage of the counselling service and its marketing to take into account a greater proportion of companies in size range of 5-50 employees and to strengthen its links with private sector organisations such as the Chambers of Commerce, Trade Associations. There may even be the potential to offer a higher level of expert 'specialisation' in services such as technical innovation, new product development, exporting, co-operation, etc. Similarly, in the provision of training, it would be possible to build on the already well developed programmes of the Training Services Division and the Training Boards into areas of comparative weakness such as provision for the very small firm (under 20 employees). This is an area of extensive provision in Germany through the Handwerkskammer and association programmes. Other opportunities lie in building into basic apprenticeship education and further education programmes the presentation of an image of possible self-employment and certain of the necessary background to encourage enterpreneurial skills. These principles are evident in certain of the German programmes. Opportunities have been noted to develop programmes aimed at provision for the existing small businessman or young man working in a small business, perhaps with a diploma qualification.

In other areas of German provision, particularly finance, support for innovation - the direction of public purchasing - more substantial change would be involved.

In the provision of finance, the basic philosophical commitment to small enterprise in West Germany is clearly underwritten in a manner which contrasts sharply with the UK. This commitment is strengthened by the universalist and regional structure of the German Banking System. For certain of the German provisions to be emulated then Britain would require obviously a recognition that capital availability is a major barrier to entry and that the start-up is capital deficient and needs to be assisted. To emulate successfully other aspects of German provision, for example, the Loan Guarantee System, would arguably require elements of local 'ownership' which have been important to the development of guarantees in Germany. And without major changes there would appear to be little prospect of commitment to subsidised interest rate finance available at both Federal and local level in Baden Wurttemberg.

In the area of support for innovation the major component missing from the UK provision compared with Baden Wurttemberg is the specialist link between sources of assistance/ideas and the firms themselves by means of expert assistance in diagnosing the problem and need. Moreover, the model of linking polytechnic and university engineering departments with small firms is absent. In the area of purchasing policy provision for the breaking up of public contracts to facilitate the small firm application, the extension of this to cases where public money is involved in private sector decisions, the encouragement of local authorities to adopt similar approaches and, most importantly, the provision of a focal specialist signposting assistance source at a regional level would all require major change in attitudes.

Major change cannot come about without major political commitment. And perhaps the clearest policy implication for the UK is at this level. The broad philosophical commitment based on the assumption that the small firms sector is 'disadvantaged' is the key that opens the door to the large number of the support measures backed by Federal and Land legislation. Such commitment begs the question as to the need in the UK for a policy overview, and to reflect on the value of the traditional stance of 'marginalist' policy.

Any review of policy might serve to take the focus away from any particular narrow short-term objective, such as, for example, employment criteria towards a wider concept. Included in this concept might be judgements about the 'balance' in society with respect to size and distribution of industry (the concentration in UK industry compared with West Germany and several other competitors); social values (the relationship of corporatism - with its conflicts - to the development of entrepreneurial middle-class values); job opportunities; the provision of alternative sources and qualities of jobs with opportunities for 'creation' of jobs by individuals; and decision-making (the weakening of centralisation of decision-making in the UK which makes it difficult for the small firm with its local orientation to articulate needs and contribute pressure of change).

Finally, it would appear indeed that it is at the regional level that there may be much to be gained by the co-ordination of small firms activities. In Baden Wurttemberg the network of small firms assistance is relatively tight: more importantly, it operates through small firm 'membership' organisations and there is clear signposting to the sources of assistance. This contrasts sharply with the weakness of membership organisations in the UK and the relatively minor role they play, overall. The plethora of assistance agencies in the UK and the considerable overlap on a regional basis contrasts sharply with the West German scheme where the only major area of duplication and competition appears to be in the financial sector. The German scene reinforces the belief that clarity of purpose and provision in small firms assistance is not synonymous with the creation of an all-purpose bureaucracy or agency but can effectively be channelled through appropriate and different local institutions for different purposes.

Overall it seems unlikely that in the present financial climate there will be much scope for many of the developments of the kind outlined above. There has been, moreover, no attempt in this paper to evaluate the real effectiveness of the assistance. Indeed, it is likely that such an attempt would be costly and difficult without necessarily yielding clear results. Nevertheless, there is a role for further research to play and a need to link with German research which is active in this field. It is doubtful, however, whether it would ever be able to provide a comprehensive answer to the key question, namely whether the UK is imbalanced in its policy commitment to the smaller business compared with many of its competitors, and whether this is of significance to the performance of the social economy.

REFERENCES

1. Ministry of Economics, Baden Wurttemberg, 'Industrial Settlement', 1978. Association of Baden Wurttemberg Chambers of Commerce, 'IHK atlas of Industrial Location', 1979. Le Moci, Moniteur du Commerce International, Baden Wurttemberg, 'comme un poisson dans l'eau'. Statistical handout of Landesgewerbeamt.

2. Ibid.

3. Ibid.

4. Law to Promote Small and Medium Sized Firms, December 16th 1978, Baden Wurttemberg.

5. Bundestag Paper 7/5248, 'Report of the Federal Government on Small Businesses', 1976 (Mittelstandbericht) May 21st 1976.

6. Federal Ministry of Economics, August 1978.

7. Op cit.

8. Sauer, Willibrord, 'The contribution of small units of enterprise to the German Economic Miracle', Acton Society Trust, Siena Services, No 13, 1978/79, Part II.

9. Official handout of Landesgewerbeamt, 1978.

10. Ministerium fur Wirtschaft, Mittelstand, 'The significance of the 'Mittelstand' - small and medium sized business'.

11. Federal Ministry of Economics, op cit, p 10.

12. Ministerium fur Wirtschaft, Mittelstand ibid, p 4.

13. Ibid, pp 3-5.

14. Federal Ministry of Economics, op cit, p 11.

15. Ibid, p 24.

16. Law to promote Small and Medium Sized Firms, op cit, p 1.

17. Federal Ministry of Economics, op cit, p 11.

18. Bannock, Graham, The Small Business in Britain and Germany (Wilton House Special Study, 1975) p 74.

19. Focusing on the academic debate following the publication of Birch, David, L, The Job Generation Process (MIT, 1979).

20. Law to promote small and medium sized firms, op cit, Section II.

21. Bannock, Graham, The Organisation of Public Sector Promotion of Small Business, Discussion Paper (Economists Advisory Group, June 1980).

22. Federal Ministry of Economics, op cit, p 27. The Promotion of small and medium sized business in Baden Wurttemberg, op cit, p 2.

23. Federal Ministry of Economics, op cit, p 24.

24. Budget of Landesgewerbeamt, 1979.

25. Data taken from Das Bankwesen in Deutschland, Fritz Knapp Verlag, Frankfurt, 1978.

26. Bundesministerium fur Wirtschaft, Das ERP Program, 1978.

27. Sauer, Willibrord, op cit, p 8.

28. Ruhnke, Hans Joachim, Director Burgschaftbank Stuttgart, Unpublished paper, 1979, p 3.

29. Ibid.

29. Ibid.

30. Bundesministerium fur Wirtschaft, op cit.

31. The report by Howndle, J M, 'An Evaluation of the Small Firms Counselling Service in the South West Region', February 1979, indicates the heavy distribution of UK small firm counselling to the start-up and very small firm.

32. By several of the clearing banks aimed at providing higher gearing for small firm start-ups.

33. Based on some preliminary findings of the research into evaluation of German innovation support schemes by the Fraunhofer Gesellschaft, Karlsruhe.

The study was financed by the UK Department of Industry whose support for the research and permission to give this paper is gratefully acknowledged. The Department has also given permission for the full report to be available.

9 Mythology and misplaced pessimism: the real failure record of new, small businesses

MICHAEL SCOTT
Newcastle upon Tyne Polytechnic

THE MYTH OUTLINED

Founding a new small firm is a very risky business. The chances of failure are high, especially in Britain. Such conventional wisdom circulates freely amongst the business community, is fostered by the media and legitimated in academic papers. Firstly, let us look at some examples of the way these views are presented.

> "'Starting money' is commonplace in motor racing. It is paid to the teams who are prepared to risk themselves and their expensive cars in beginning a highly dangerous venture. The prize money is, after all, a distant prospect for most, and many of them will not finish the race anyway. The parallel with new business enterprises is obvious ..."(1)

> "Three-quarters of new businesses don't survive the first 2 years."(2)

> "It is not surprising that a high proportion of entrepreneurs cannot stay the pace. Business mortality

figures vary, but according to one study more than 70% of all business failures occur within the first 10 years and more than 60% within the first five."(3)

"You're reading this book because you want to know more about starting (or buying) and operating your own business. You're taking a step that will increase your chances of success. Approximately 10,000 known business failures and discontinuations occur each year: many more are unrecorded."(4)

"Many small businesses die in their infancy. In fact, of the 500,000 new businesses born each year in the US, only half live as long as 18 months and only 1 in 5 lives as long as 10 years."(5)

"Each year, over 400,000 small businesses fail, costing the taxpayer more than $4.4 billion in liabilities and lost revenue ... Most people starting a new business are sincere and dedicated. Usually they bring a special art or skill with them, and a willingness to work long hours. Yet in two years, half of all these new businesses will be down the drain."(6)

"A comparison with other industrialised countries ... shows how badly the UK has suffered in the contraction of its small manufacturing sector ... At the smallest level of less than 10 employees there are only about 27,000 manufacturers in this country compared with 180,000 in

France and 150,000 in Germany. Furthermore the difference is getting rapidly worse, with a considerably higher 'death rate' and a 'birth rate' of only about one third of some other industrial countries."(7)

These extracts have been chosen as being indicative of the way business failure is treated. The reader is invited to check his own bookshelf and files where he will no doubt discover similar statements. Certain common features in all these are worth examining:

i. Inconsistencies in data presentation. 'Failure' is expressed in a variety of ways, eg. as aggregate totals of discontinued businesses in a single year or as statements of life expectancy. Given variability across time and from place to place, unless such data is presented precisely, it becomes fudged, suspect and inconsistent - as in the examples given. In particular, data produced in one country are somehow assumed to be perfectly transferable to others.

ii. Imprecision in terminology. The following words appear to be almost universally interchangeable - 'failure', 'death', 'discontinued', 'bankrupt'. A separate paper would be required to examine these definitional problems, but common sense will indicate that these terms do not mean the same thing. In the case of 'failure', for instance, we have to be clear whether our level of analysis is the single individual or the whole economy. As David Watkins says "The proportion of new businesses that succeed depends very much on how the proprietor defines 'success' - in other words, by what one defines as one's objective when establishing a new firm."(8) The often loose way in which 'failed' and 'bankrupt' are used synonymously is a special case of this imprecision, firstly because there is evidence that only a small proportion of discontinued businesses involve bankruptcy(9), and secondly because of the moral undertone associated with the word bankrupt itself.

iii. The tone of the statements. The metaphors used are often concerned with 'risk', 'failure' and 'death'. Starting a new business, it would seem, is almost evidence of a Captain Oates' syndrome!

THE NATURE OF THE EVIDENCE AND ITS MISUSE

We know very little about the dynamics of the small business sector in the UK, ie. we do not know accurately what the total stock of small firms is(10), how many new firms enter each year, nor how many cease to trade or for what reasons they cease to trade. This ignorance enables policy-making to go on unhindered by reference to nasty 'facts'(11).

In respect of business failure and discontinuation, the following sources of information are worth examination: Dun and Bradstreet's 'Business Failure Record', other US Sources, and United Kingdom data.

i) Dun and Bradstreet's 'Business Failure Record'. This annual US publication(12) is perhaps the most frequently quoted (and misquoted) source of failure statistics. The tables particularly of relevance are:

Table 1: Failure Trends Since 1920 (extracts)

Year	No of failures	Total failure liabilities $	Failure rate per 10,000 listed concerns	Average liability per failure $
1920	8,881	295,121,000	48	33,230
1930	26,355	668,282,000	122	25,357
1960	15,445	938,630,000	57	60,772
1970	10,748	1,887,754,000	44	175,638
1978	6,619	2,656,006,000	24	401,270

Table 2: Failure Distribution by Liability Size (extracts)

Year	under $5000 %	$5-25,000 %	$25-100,000 %	$100,000-1m %	Over $1m %
1960	10.9	44.6	32.9	11.0	0.6
1970	4.0	29.7	40.9	22.8	2.6
1978	1.2	14.0	40.9	39.2	4.7

Table 3: Age of Failed Businesses 1978 (extracts)

Age in Years	Manufacturing %	Wholesale %	Retail %	Construction %	Service %	All Concerns %
less than 1	0.9	0.6	1.4	0.5	0.9	1.0
1 to 2	10.6	7.2	13.6	6.4	7.8	10.5
2 to 3	13.6	14.7	19.1	13.6	16.0	16.4
Total 3 or less	25.1	22.5	34.1	20.5	24.7	27.9
Total 5 or less	47.3	48.8	60.2	45.7	51.1	53.2
Total 6-10	26.2	25.8	25.4	33.4	28.9	27.4
Over 10	26.5	25.4	14.4	20.9	20.0	19.4
No of failures	1013	740	2889	1204	773	6619

Table 4: Failure Age Trend (extracts)

Year	% in Business 5 years or less	% in Business 6-10 years	% in Business Over 10 years
1950	68.2	19.0	12.8
1960	58.6	20.8	20.6
1970	54.9	22.7	22.4
1978	53.2	27.4	19.4

It has been alleged that these figures are misinterpreted to give rise to 3 'myths' about business failure(13).

1. Dun & Bradstreet's Rate of Failure statistics indicate a high mortality rate in business enterprises
2. Dun & Bradstreet states that the mortality rate among small businesses is greater than among large businesses
3. Dun & Bradstreet reports that a large per cent of all firms fail during the early years(14).

The source of the first myth is simple misinterpretation of the data, ie. Table 3 is taken as evidence that, say, 53.2% of all firms fail within 5 years. In fact, the correct interpretation is, that of those firms which failed in 1978, 53.2% were under 5 years old. Since the Dun & Bradstreet records covered approximately 2,758,000 firms in the year, the actual rate of failure for all firms was a quarter of one per cent (0.24%), scarcely a "high mortality rate". The catch, of course, is that "failure" here only includes bankruptcy, or ceasing trading with a loss to creditors, or as a result of court action. There are many times more instances of business "discontinuances" but these are not reported by Dun & Bradstreet: they merely report that over 5000 changes are made every business day in their listings, and "this is all evidence of the dynamic change and turnover constantly taking place in the business population". In sum, as Dun & Bradstreet state clearly, "failures do not represent total business discontinuances".

The second myth arises from a misinterpretation of Table 2, ie. since 56.1% of firms failed with liabilities of less than $100,000, it is assumed that this must refer to small firms. Since Dun & Bradstreet do no analysis of their data in terms of other measures of size, such as number of employees, sales or fixed assets, one simply cannot make such assumptions validly. Note also that in these figures liabilities do not mean loss, since offsetting assets are disregarded! An American Government enquiry in 1973 in fact concluded "In sum, the commonly supposed relationship between size and failure, that the larger the firm, the less likely it is to fail, received but small confirmation in the Commission study"(15).

The third myth arises, as indicated earlier, from an assumption that the sample of failed businesses is a predictor for the total population of enterprises. Unfortunately, we simply do not know whether it is or not in the absence of either an age breakdown of the population or an age profile of US industry. Additionally, "the ages of the firms appearing in the Dun & Bradstreet distribution of failures are suspect. A successor firm which takes over from a predecessor firm is not really comparable to one that began from age zero and had to assemble employees, customers, suppliers and money"(16).

Finally, if in addition to all the foregoing we take account of the fact that Dun & Bradstreet do not include in their figures the following businesses - financial enterprises (including banks, mortgage, loan and investment companies) insurance and real estate companies, railroads, terminals, amusements, many small one-man services, the professions or farming - it would seem that the Business Failure Record is of questionable value, despite its apparent popularity. For the United Kingdom it would seem of no practical use - which is essentially what the Bolton Report indicated(17).

(ii) Other US Sources. The Bolton Committee also came to the conclusion that other US statistical series (which showed that as many as 8% of all operating businesses were discontinued each year at the beginning of the 1970s) were too broad "to permit any valid comparisons to be made with this country".

This raises the question of whether the recent, and influential, Birch Report(18) should be included in Bolton's 'not relevant here' category. For it does appear to contain strong evidence that "the odds of an establishment dying over a 7 year period are quite high". And the data are presented in terms of size (number of employees) so we can examine the mortality of small firms of differing ages: see Table 5.

Table 5: Components of Change by Age and Size for Establishments in the US 1969-75 (extract)

Size	Age (yrs)	Expand (%)	Contract(%)	Die (%)	Total
0-20 employees	0-4	27.6	7.6	64.8	503,406
	5-9	32.7	10.4	56.9	372,897
	10+	33.4	12.5	54.1	882,762
	Totals	31.6	10.7	57.8	1,759,065

We do not know, of course, to what extent this picture might be relevant to the UK. An attempt to compare the job generation aspects of the study with UK data(19) concluded that there were areas of broad comparability, although strict comparisons were not possible because of heavy emphasis in Birch on service sector enterprises. Fothergill and Gudgin comment:

"The inclusion of the service sector, in particular, will boost the importance of new and small firms in two ways. Firstly, the rate of firm birth (and firm closure) is far higher in services. Secondly, the secular growth of the share of total employment in services will boost the importance of small firms in the US economy as a whole simply because the average firm in services is much smaller than in manufacturing. As the demand for services grows, existing small enterprises will expand, and more room will be created for new, small service firms. The result will be a massive growth of employment in small business. What Birch observes is a consequence, not a cause, of economic development, as employment in advanced industrial countries shifts away from manufacturing and into services."(20)

It may be doubted whether the UK has such dynamism in its service sector, with easy entry, high birth rates for new enterprises, and rates of death comparable to those given in the Birch study. Further, the notion of 'failure' has to be related to the level of analysis, as indicated earlier. If the drug store on main street changes hands every year, this may represent 'failure' in the statistics (and even on a personal level) but need not mean this for the community - it may spell improvement.

Until adequate data is available for the UK, it is clearly advisable to treat imported US data on failure rates with a great deal of caution.

(iii) United Kingdom Data. The considered opinion of the Bolton Committee was that "Roughly speaking, it may be said that between 1 and 2 per cent of companies in Great Britain die each year due to failure. (Note: Failure is defined broadly to include the formation of companies that never begin trading and are later disbanded!) Nothing is known explicitly about the failures of unincorporated firms but, since they are generally smaller than companies, we can only presume (from what is known about the relation between failure and size) that the failure rate for unincorporated firms would be higher."(21)

No further data were available to indicate the size or age distribution of failures. However, and very importantly, the Committee points out elsewhere:

> "A very large proportion of the numbers of small firms that cease independent trading each year do so through being acquired by other firms. According to the Merrett Cyriax Survey, Research Report No 12, over half of the firms in manufacturing which left the small firms population sample in 1963 did so through being taken over."(22)

Recent evidence by Smith would appear to support this view of the importance of take overs for the demise of small firms, at least in the Northern Region.

> "That it is the small firm which is primarily involved in the acquisition process, is suggested by evidence compiled from local press reports in the Northern region. Almost 60%

of externally-acquired indigenous manufacturing companies, between 1963 and 1973, were small private concerns, with an issued capital of less than £200,000 (this probably considerably understates the true proportion as a substantial number of small takeovers are not even reported in the local press). Further 'other evidence suggests that the typical acquired firm is far from being the 'lame duck' which the conventional wisdom would have us believe ... The majority of these firms appeared to be characterised by satisfactory profit positions and good management records.'"(23)

It would appear therefore that less than 2% of companies 'die' each year (but some of these never start to trade) and possibly more than 2% of unincorporated businesses. Half or more of these are taken over, and probably cannot be regarded as failures anyway. We do not know anything about the age distribution of these discontinued companies and so cannot say whether a new firm is more or less liable to failure. The other published statistics are of little help to us. New company registrations are running at about 65,000 per year, of which around 96% have an issued nominal capital of less than £100,000(24). Company liquidations total about 5000 a year(25) but these are not disaggregated by size, nor are they likely to be representative of business failures as a whole. The total number of companies on the register at 31.12.78 was effectively 692,186(26).

At this point we have to begin grasping at straws. For instance, the Wilson Committee suggest that the number of small firms has reached a plateau, with a rise in manufacturing, a small decline in construction and a rapid decline in retailing(27). The implication of a fixed stock of course is that discontinuations equal starts (about which we have no data!). Secondly, there is tentative evidence that it is second generation businesses with succession problems which are particularly prone to failure(28).

To summarise so far.

- We know little about the dynamics of the small firm sector.
- United States data are unhelpful and have, through misinterpretation, led to an overstated view of the risks entailed in new enterprise formation.
- A small percentage, probably in single figures, of the total business stock suffers discontinuance in any year. For small firms, this is often through take-over, and may not represent failure.
- We have no information on specifically new firms, and while they obviously are at risk, we don't know whether they are disproportionately at risk, when compared to, say, second generation firms.

RECENT BRITISH EVIDENCE

Scottish Company Data

At this point, it is appropriate to introduce some new data. These are based on an analysis of the records of all Scottish companies registered in 1969. These totalled 935. Information is held by the Registrar of Companies on their main activities, address and date of incorporation. From these, a small sample of 37 new, independent companies were the subject of detailed investigation and interview in 1970-71(29). In 1977 a follow-up(30) was carried out as follows:

i) the Registrar of Companies Records in Edinburgh were again inspected and in particular data were obtained on:

a) whether the company was still on the register, or had been liquidated or withdrawn (and, if so, at what date and for what reason)

b) whether trading accounts, or annual reports, or no-trading certificates were filed.

ii) postal questionnaires were sent to all 935 companies and 201 replies were received. This gives a crude response rate of 22.4%, but it should be noted that by 1977, 264 companies had been removed from the register, and of the remaining 671, only 458 appeared to be active in the sense of having filed (around 1977) their 1975 reports and/or accounts. An estimated response rate of 201: 458 or 43.8% is therefore more apprpriate.

iii) attempts were made to trace as many as possible of the original founders previously interviewed, and carry out a follow-up interview, primarily to establish the company's progress, or the reasons for its failure. Tracing proved possible in 33 cases, although it was only feasible to arrange further interviews with 15 cases.

The Main Findings

i) Registrar of Companies Data

Records are kept for each company which registers in two basic forms: a brief summary record of the main events (such as change of directors, filing of reports or changes of legal status) and an individual file for each company where all documents are kept. It is, therefore, possible to extract information of a general nature (eg. has the company been filing annual returns regularly) without having to inspect the detailed files for each company. The follow-up data were mainly of this general form, and for the purposes of analysis, each company was coded for every year as follows:

1. Probably trading, ie. annual returns and accounts filed for the year, and/or other substantial activity on the file to indicate trading.

2. Not trading, ie. a certificate of 'no-trading' was filed with the registrar, or in some cases equivalent evidence by correspondence.

3. Liquidated or removed from the register.

4. Last accounts filed in this year.

5. Annual reports filed but no accounts. This usually implies that trading is taking place, and accounts are often subsequently filed (companies are notorioously late in filing accounts and this may be because of accounting difficulties or taxation issues).

Additionally, where companies were liquidated, or removed from the register, data were obtained on the date of final notice of removal, or in the case of liquidation, the date of creditors, members or court meetings (the actual date of removal from the register was not recorded as this is largely governed by bureaucratic procedures in the Registrar's office).

Recording was done in 1977, and it may be assumed that data for the years up to 1974 and probably 1975 are accurate. Since companies often take 2 years from the end of their financial year to file accounts, etc, it may be assumed that 1976 and 1977 data are not accurate.

a) Number of Years Trading

Table 6 shows the aggregate trading record of the 935 companies registered in 1969.

From this it can be seen that nearly a quarter of companies never traded or filed reports. From other evidence it is clear that many were legal contrivances of one form or another, never intending to trade and often set up for taxation purposes. Secondly, it may be surprising that

Table 6

	No	%
Traded* for under 5 years	152	16
Traded* 5-7 years	408	43
Traded* 8 years	157	17
Never traded or no returns	218	23
	935	99

*Only includes cases where returns or accounts filed

so many companies have long trading records, ie. the amount of activity is substantial, with 60% of companies trading for more than 5 years.

b) Trading Records Throughout the Years

Table 7 sets out the aggregate data for each recorded year. The 'probably trading' column represents the best estimate that can be made, and includes companies filing regular accounts and/or reports. The 'balance' column represents the total trading at 1st January of the previous year less liquidations or removals during that year. It may be regarded as a running "live cases" balance.

This table would seem to dispel some of the earlier stated mythology about the alleged short life of new companies. For instance, of the 935 original companies, 713 were apparently trading in some form in 1969, and after 5 years, in 1973, 699 companies were trading. These are not necessarily the same companies (since some of the 713 will have been

Table 7

Year	Probably trading	Liquidated or removal	Balance at year end	Trading as % of balance	Not trading	Not trading as % of balance
1969	713	5	930	76.2	79	8.4
1970	722	14	916	77.6	78	8.3
1971	720	23	893	78.6	80	8.7
1972	694	37	856	77.7	81	9.0
1973	659	41	815	76.9	74	8.6
1974	598	37	778	73.3	70	8.5
1975	458	28	750	58.8	69	8.8

liquidated, and others not trading in 1969 will have commenced later) but the figures do not indicate any dramatic fall in activity. The number of liquidations is never more than 6.2% of the total trading in any year, and even if we assume that those companies for which information is not available are in fact not trading (an unlikely situation), it appears almost as a constant (Col 5) that three-quarters of the balance remaining in any year will be trading. The general conclusion to be drawn from this table would be that companies which intended to trade, and actually started to trade, had a strong likelihood of remaining in business at least for 5 years, and in many cases for the whole period of recording.

c) Liquidations

The reasons for removal from the Register are set out in Table 8.

Table 8

	No		%
No returns filed, removed by Registrar	190		72
Liquidated: members resolution	22)		
creditors resolution	33)	68	26
court action	13)		
Under notice of removal by Registrar	3)		
Provisional liquidators assigned	3)	6	2
	264		100

= 28.2% of original 935 after approximately 9 years

Again the evidence of these figures is that the rate of removal of companies from the Register is not such as to support the myth of the high initial mortality of new companies.

ii) Questionnaire Data

Questionnaires were sent to all 935 companies, and 201 were returned, of which 60 were not usable (7 were charitable 'old peoples homes' which happened to register in 1969, and the remainder were either returned blank or marked "return to sender"). The data below are therefore based on 141 usable replies.

Companies were asked to indicate whether they were trading in the years 1969-77 inclusive. The results are given in Table 9.

These results tally well with the Registrar's data, ie. over 60% of companies registered in 1969 were trading 9 years later. These results can be assumed to be unrepresentative in some measure since companies which are 'live' may be more likely to reply to a questionnaire.

Table 9

	Numbers Trading	%
1969	77	54.6
1970	96	68.0
1971	97	68.7
1972	96	68.0
1973	93	65.9
1974	90	63.8
1975	91	64.5
1976	90	63.8
1977	89	63.1

Nonetheless they do indicate that survival is a feature of these companies.

iii) Interview Data

It was found that (as in both the Registrar's data and the questionnaire data) about 60% of the companies continued to trade after 9 years. What is particularly interesting is the fact that over half of the failed cases provide instances where one of the original founders has gone on to start or run another business, which all appear to be themselves surviving. One of the main findings of the original research was that a stimulus to entrepreneurial activity was a need for independence and antagonism towards large scale organisations. This follow-up suggests that 'once an entrepreneur, always an entrepreneur', even when the first attempt fails.

The casualties are not randomly distributed: the companies founded on a part-time basis, and those with innovation as an important part of their work, were particularly vulnerable. The most striking group of successes are those companies whose founders were formerly in large organisations and whose original reason for founding was because of blocked promotion or the threat of removal from Scotland. The (untested) implication of these successes (there are no failures amongst this group) is that large company experience in professional or managerial roles is a training ground for entrepreneurs.

What are the implications of the foregoing data? Firstly, that it would be dangerous to read too much into one restricted set of findings with obvious methodological problems. For instance, the companies studied will not be fully representative of all Scottish companies, and one can hypothesise that the very process of registration demands a level of business knowledge and planning not necessarily to be found in the establishment of unincorporated companies or partnerships; and that therefore these companies ought to be the more successful. However, the overall results which show a good majority of companies surviving even after 6 and 7 years, are so at variance with the conventional wisdom and myths surrounding the alleged failure rates of new enterprises, that they ought at the very least make us think again. What we need, it is suggested, is more data from cohort studies of new businesses.

Other Current Evidence

Business Schools and Colleges of Higher Education throughout the UK are currently providing, under the aegis of the Manpower Services

Commission, Training Services Division, courses for entrepreneurs about to start up new businesses. To the 9th May 1980, these schemes (New Enterprise Programmes and Small Business Courses) had enrolled 597 students, in 48 different programmes. The number of known businesses set up as a result of this activity was 339. No information is presently available about the number of failures, but it is understood that a rolling 3 year evaluation programme (ie. a check on course participants 3 years after completion) has now commenced, so that in future failure rates should be fairly accurately determinable. At present, only anecdotal information from Training Services Division staff is available, but it is clear that failure rates are low, and there is certainly no support for the mythology set out in the earlier part of this paper.

There is indicative information, therefore, that the failure rates of newly established businesses do not correspond to current conventional wisdom and that high propensity to failure is a myth.

THE DANGERS OF MYTH CREATION AND THEIR IMPLICATIONS

Myths represent an attempt to cope with uncertainty, to impose an 'explanation' of the complexity which surrounds us: a 'simplifying' expedient. They thus share some common features with the scientific hypothesis. The latter is however subject to empirical testing by objective data, and should be self-correcting. The myth never is, and assumes the status of religious faith. The danger is that believers, acting in the faith, may take actions which have unintended consequences in the real world.

Racial 'myths' are a useful example of this process. For instance, the contemporary civil disturbances in Northern Ireland provide the outsider, and especially the English, with a bewilderingly complex view of a set of political, religious and criminal actions, whose underlying history and motives he does not understand. So a simplifying myth is created, based on the assumption that the violence, since it cannot be comprehended, must be 'mindless'. Therefore it must be the product of stupid individuals. Hence the popularity of 'Irish' jokes which have the sole common feature of portraying Irishmen as 'thick', and which serve to keep the myth fresh. It need not be emphasised that policy decisions based on such a myth would be suspect.

The myth that new small businesses are doomed to early failure, whilst it may have some positive aspects, similarly may give rise to policies which are counter productive. This is particularly true in the matter of financial provision. The Wilson Committee drew attention to this problem in their discussion of the banking sector as a provider of funds for the small business:

> "Their attitude towards risk, and ability to assess it, are said to make them unnecessarily restrictive in their lending policy, particularly towards new or rapidly expanding small firms."(31)

> "A final justification for the banks' attitude to security ... Is their belief that lending to small firms is more risky than lending to large and that loss ratios are therefore likely to be higher. Unfortunately they do not

> appear to keep their records in a way which would make it possible to demonstrate conclusively that this is the case. Data about bad debt experience are generally analysed by industrial sector, or size of loan, rather than by size of customer."(32)

Here surely is the myth operating to produce policies adverse to the development of new businesses. And note the self-fulfilling nature of the mythology, which is not subjected to any checking process.

The Wilson Committee implicate, in an indirect way, the media's role in this process, in their discussion of the encouragement of new forms of co-operative ventures:

> "our impression is that the well publicised failure of some of these enterprises has led traditional sources of finance to approach many worthwhile co-operative projects requiring start up capital with excessive caution."(33)

Since the mythology operates within the banks, one can but speculate that it operates elsewhere: amongst those providing premises, goods on credit, labour, and of course potential customers. How many decisions, crucial to the new business venture, are coloured by the myth "Well, he probably won't survive for long anyway"?

To be fair, myths may also perform useful functions, and one can envisage that the myth of high failure may

i) act as an awful warning to those contemplating starting up, so that they think hard about their venture. This self-filtering process is clearly necessary, but the issue is, how fine a filter is being used? The mythology may lead to self filters of a mesh size far below what would in fact lead to success.

ii) act as a caution to those supplying goods and services to new ventures, so that they demand evidence of substance or commitment from the entrepreneur. The suggestion is that potential entrepreneurs need hurdles to test their stamina, and that taking away all difficulties would enable flabby candidates for certain failure to enter the race. The problem is that we do not know how many hurdles there need to be, nor how high to make them.

iii) act as a support to the 'macho' of existing entrepreneurs, or provide evidence that the rites of passage into the small business community are sufficiently strenuous. This may give rise to self-help and co-operation within that community.

These are useful functions, and the value judgement to be made is: do they outweigh the dysfunctional effect of bad policy decisions described earlier? One would like to see some more facts before making that value judgement.

REFERENCES

1. Gorb, P, 'Starting Money', The Accountant, Feb 21, 1980, pp 265-267.

2. 'Can we make jobs' Programme 1, BBC, 6 Aug 1980.

3. Tisdall, P, 'Aunt Agatha's legacy is sadly missed', Times, Special Report, 17 April 1980, p 1.

4. Franz, F H, Successful Small Business Management, Prentice Hall, NJ, 1978, p 3.

5. Siropolis, N C, Small Business Management, Houghton Mifflin, Boston, 1977, p 9.

6. Soloman, G T and Whiting, B G, 'Casualities of Ignorance: the dilemma of small businesses in the USA', Acton Society Trust, Siena Series, 1977/9, No 16.

7. Davis, J D, Springboards for Small Enterprises, Intermediate Technology Development Group, Cambridge, no date.

8. Watkins, D, Starting in Business: a guide for small firms, Small Firms Information Centres Publication 1, 1973.

9. Donleavy, D, Small Business Guardian, 1 Feb 1980.

10. See Financing of Small Firms, interim report of the 'Wilson Committee', 1979, Cmnd 7503, Appendix 2. Note the references to "unsatisfactory" data.

11. Note the alacrity with which the Birch Report was used to legitimate existing government policy in support of the small firms sector. It has been suggested that if Birch did not exist, the Small Business lobby would have had to invent him. Less publicity has been accorded a study which attempted to replicate Birch's work in the UK and which stated: "it would be a disaster if Birch's conclusions and recommendations - that we should abandon assistance to larger known corporations - were to become the basis of British industrial policy". Fothergill, S and Gudgin, G, 'The Job Generation process in Britain', CES Research Series 32, Nov 1979, p 22.

12. Business Economics Division, Dun & Bradstreet Corporation, 99 Church St, New York NY10007, Reference here is to 1979 edition.

13. Massel, M Z, 'It's Easier to slay a dragon than kill a myth', Journal Small Business Management 16, No 3, 1978, pp 44-49. I am indebted to Mike Massel for several of the ideas contained in this paper.

14. Ibid, p 45.

15. Fredland, J E, 'The Business Bankrupts', Report of the Commission on the Bankruptcy Laws of the United States Part III, US Congress, House of Representatives, July 1973, p 6.

16. Ibid, p 48.

17. Bolton, J E, Report of the Committee of Inquiry on Small Firms, p 74, Cmnd 4811, HMSO 1971.

18. Birch, D L, The Job Generation Process, MIT Programme on Neighborhood and Regional Change, Cambridge, Mass, 1979.

19. Fothergill, S and Gudgin, G, op cit.

20. Ibid, p 20.

21. Bolton Report, op cit, p 73.

22. Ibid, p 10.

23. Smith, I J, 'The Effect of External Takeovers on Manufacturing employment change in the Northern Region between 1963 and 1973', Regional Studies 13, 1979.

24. See Trade and Industry, 26 Jan 1979, p 163 for company registrations since 1945.

25. See British Business, 30 May 1980, p 71 for insolvency records since 1968.

26. See British Business, 16 March 1979, p 561.

27. Op cit, p 2.

28. See Merrett Cyriax Associates, Dynamics of Small Firms, Research Report No 12, Committee of Inquiry on Small Firms, 1971, Founder managed, first generation firms tend to achieve rates of growth which are 2 or 3 times greater than successive generation firms.

29. See Scott, M G, 'Independence and the flight from large scale' in Gibb, A and Webb, T (eds) Policy Issues in Small Business Research, Saxon House, 1980.

30. The following tables and discussion are taken from Scott, M G, Final Report to SSRC, Grant HR4868/2, Jan 1980.

31. Wilson Committee, op cit, Chap 4, para 3.

32. Ibid, Chap 4, para 11. The article with which this paper began makes an interesting further comment. "Yet if most new start-ups fail why then are the banks still solvent? They do not reveal their losses on 'starting money' but I am prepared to bet that they are acceptably low. Nor, in spite of the banks' insistence on personal collateral on start up loans, do we hear of failed entrepreneurs being turned out of their houses in their thousands."

33. Ibid, p 22, para 63.

10 Family and business: inside the small hotel

JOHN HAYES
Preston Polytechnic

BACKGROUND

Studies relating to entrepreneurs have often been constructed around the emergence of the superhero of fact and fiction, who goes off into the economic jungle alone, and is rewarded or punished for his ability or inadequacy in coping with the opportunities and challenges he finds there.

Why, then, concern ourselves here with the family? Perhaps because this study, albeit in an industry dominated by family organisations, has elicited evidence of the kind of limitless energy and endurance of the human spirit: amputated toes, arthritic joints, suppression of pre-natal pains until chores were complete, and a general enthusiasm for work which political leaders have long been striving to inculcate into our society. What special form of organisation produces these effects? Are they due to the inspiration of our hero? Is he a special breed? Does he really exist at all?

Face to face, there is nothing remarkable in the make-up of the proprietors in this survey. They watch television as I do, have a flutter on the horses, etc. What is perhaps unique is that the family -

father, mother, sister, uncle, aunt, etc. - are en masse at the workface. What greater incentive to work is there than to avoid the wrath of mother-in-law!

The hotel and catering industry is a very important employer, investor and earner of overseas currency. But it is dominated by the small unit run by families and, on the evidence of this study, is likely to remain so. The following extract from a Hotel and Catering EDC publication(1) illustrates this industrial structure.

British Hotels - 1 January 1974

				Bedrooms			
	4-10	11-15	16-25	26-50	51-100	Over 100	Total
(000)	20.7	6.7	3.0	2.0	0.9	0.4	33.7
(%)	61.4	19.9	8.9	5.9	3.7	0.2	100.0

But the Hotel and Catering industry is by no means the only one in which tightly held family concerns exist. Thus an understanding of the mechanisms which affect the motivations and expectations of key decision-makers of this industry may have important lessons for us in other fields. Moreover, rather than being a structural throwback, they may presage new forms of industrial structure; for, in a period of economic stress, when more and more are being laid off and are in receipt of redundancy money, the acquisition of a property with rooms to let for visitors may seem a sensible move. As Handy(2) recently wrote "I actually see the new work opportunities for clean, semi-skilled work playing into the hands of women .... I think that women are more flexible, but men are more powerful. Men are so manipulative, they may well make it fashionable to be a househusband ... though they won't use that word". Perhaps in the future one will be able to add to those industries in which the family directly plays a significant role - such as retailing and farming. This paper will have served its purpose if the centre of the entrepreneurial stage is occupied, if only for a brief space, by the family.

THE HOTEL DEFINED

A hotel is an establishment which provides accommodation and food for travellers and temporary residents. A private house can, on occasion, meet these requirements - the parental admonishment to a teenager often ends with "you treat this place like a hotel!" However, there are Acts of Parliament which define a hotel.

The Hotel Proprietors Act (1956) defined a hotel as "an establishment held out by the proprietor as offering food, drink and if so required, sleeping accommodation, without special contract to any traveller presenting himself who appears able and willing to pay a reasonable sum for services required, and who is in a fit state to be received". There are, in addition, establishments which provide hotel services for residents only by contract, and are referred to as 'Private Hotels'.

The term 'hotel' can be used in this country without any legal implications. Each proprietor can decide whether his establishment shall operate within the 1956 Act or not. Some establishments mainly provide meals and bar facilities with a few rooms available for guests, "these may be vigorously called an hotel, an inn, a public house or the like"(3). Other agencies, for example the Catering Wages Commission, suggest that four letting bedrooms (or accommodation for eight guests) is the minimum to be a residential unit. This criterion is also used to define a guest house or boarding house. Finally, the Fire Precautions (Hotels and Boarding Houses) Order 1972 is concerned only with properties providing sleeping facilities for a minimum of six persons, which includes both guests and staff.

CONCEPTUAL FRAMEWORK AND METHODOLOGY

We shall find that inns, public hotels, private hotels and guest houses compete with each other for customers. Their mechanisms for survival and growth are connected with the mutual selection process of accommodation establishment and client. Matches are continually being made and, for some, go on 'until death do us part'.

This process is similar to the effect of a stone thrown into a pool, making a series of widening circles. The inner ring comprises the founder-members of the business (usually a husband and wife), the next ring is the extended family, a further ring, trusted employees, and the outer ring the regular clientele of the business who return year after year to the same resort, same hotel, same room, same time of year - the whole process interacting yet held together almost as a family. After all Harris(4) reminds us: "whatever we mean by the term family, it is not, and cannot be, an exclusive kin category of people". In fact, the familiar family is, in academic terms, somewhat under-researched.

As Bott(5) writes "the family is the backbone of society. But, actually not much is known of the relationships between families and society. There are very few studies of the way families interact with external person and institutions and there are not even very many studies of families in their natural habitat, the home".

This study then is concerned with such an interaction: one brought about by the entrepreneurial venture of the family simultaneously at work and at home in an industry where there is considerable domestic and industrial role congruence.

Any research involving organisational development must take into account the work of contingency theorists. A model of the family firm was initially developed using some of these concepts. An interview schedule was then constructed around it, so that respondents would concern themselves with factors such as inputs, tasks, task structures, task relations, environment and output while using their own words to express their experiences.

In effect, the contingency model enabled the data to be classified under general headings, but the information only made sense within the context of family issues. The emergent theme of this study, therefore, became the family within the environment of the hotel.

The field study was restricted to two environments, Lakeland and Fylde, and to hotels with between 11 and 50 letting bedrooms. This represents a significant slice of the hotel industry and provided interesting comparisons, from solo operations run by a housewife to a 3-star hotel with a large staff. In addition, it was considered important to study businesses in different stages of development, and three artificial categories were devised initially to group the hoteliers.

(a) Initiates (less than 3 seasons)

(b) Developers (between 3 and 10 seasons)

(c) Established (more than 10 seasons)

This resulted in the following sample being used:-

Rooms	11-15	16-25	26-50	Total
Initiates	19	15	5	39
Developers	24	21	7	52
Established	20	22	15	57
	63	58	27	148

The findings suggest the following patterns of development:

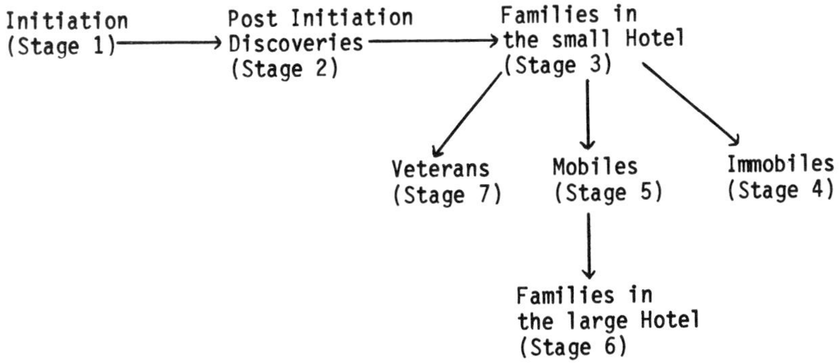

Small hotels are those between 11 and 15 letting bedrooms. Immobiles are families who have remained in the original acquisition for at least 10 seasons. Mobiles are those who have owned more than one hotel or guest house consecutively. Large hotels are between 26-50 letting bedrooms, and Veterans are those contemplating retirement, or about to retire.

This paper will be confined to a discussion of some aspects of the findings only, namely the Initiate families in small hotels, and some aspects of mobility and immobility.

THE INITIATE

It is difficult to envisage every guest house and small hotel in every tourist environment in the UK housing an entrepreneur in the classical sense, but the building provides a roof for a family and that family unit can be self-supporting. What better way is there of supporting the principal breadwinner of the household who is in some occupation in the area? It may pay the family to move to a holiday environment to set up such an arrangement.

There is no single reason for families coming into the business, but seven major categories were identified in the study.

- A role for the wife, and a domicile
- A major family event, resulting in a change of job or location
- Family factors, divorce, widowhood, etc
- Redundancy, semi-retirement, loss of interest in job
- An extension of entrepreneurial activity or activities
- Fulfilment of professional ambitions
- Investment reasons

The manner of purchasing the initial hotel varies considerably. The deliberations of the professional may involve the use of a check-list similar to those outlined by Quest(6) but, for many, the process of acquisition is an unhappy event. Stories of bad advice from solicitors, bankers and estate agencies abound. Interviews included references to Dutch auctions, gazumping, last-minute bids by telegram, the rush to get a signature on the contract, etc. There was often evidence or suggestion of shady dealing: "The bloke who sold said his books were with the accountant. The bank was not interested in his accounts, took everything at face value (when arranging the loan). Everyone in the resort thought it was a flourishing business ... the previous owner would buy 50 tins of this and that at exhibitions in the town, just to impress ... we have an office full of pineapple chunks". Caveat emptor would seem to be the cardinal principle to follow in any dealings involving property by any family; much more so in the dual context of business and family.

Once this initial hurdle has been dealt with the new broom is evidently quickly in use. The emphasis throughout is on bringing the hotel "up to our standards" ... "would be ashamed to let visitors in now!"

As Quest(6) observes: "(Hotelkeeping) ... is an immensely personal activity in which the hotelier expresses his own individuality through his hotel and the way he runs it". Part of the success of the inspired amateur is due therefore to the re-creation of a home-from-home atmosphere. This led one of the American respondents interviewed during the study to say:

> "I admire two of your national institutions, the guest house where you can get a decent bed and breakfast, and the Queen" (presumably in order of merit!)

Much of Quest's(6) advice seems to be directed to husbands and wives contemplating hotel purchase. The evidence of this study suggests that there are, especially in the initial stages, many solo operations run mainly by women. Gove suggests one reason why this may be so:

"The married woman's structural base is typically more fragile than is the man's. Women generally occupy only one major social role ... men occupy two ... household head and worker"(7). The man can, therefore, switch roles if one is not particularly satisfying. The small hotel or guest house can provide an outlet in which the married woman can fulfil her perceived obligations to her husband and children and, at the same time, gain some objective economic recognition for what she does as a housewife.

Domestic roles can become highly segregated in such operations with the wife running the business and the husband in employment but giving help and encouragement. The business becomes "the wife's domain" ... "her life" ... "her hobby" etc; in some cases the husband only reluctantly gives a hand.

For once, the technology of an industry operates in favour of the female members of society. Dennis, Henriques and Slaughter(8) have described the role of the miner's wife: "Miners expect their wives to feed them and look after them when they are out of the tense mining situation, but to be as undemanding as possible". The Hotel and Catering industry is quite different for, as Walton says, "Even when the husband was on the premises, ... lodging-house keeping was very much a women's business. Blackpool became full of men who were primarily landladies' husbands, doing odd jobs or taking seasonal work"(10). Walton was writing about behaviour patterns at the turn of the century, but today the importance of the feminine role cannot be underestimated and has been little affected by those technical changes which have taken place.

Normal modes of family organisation are reflected in business organisation. Bott has distinguished three modes of domestic management: (a) complementary, (b) independent and (c) joint organisation(5). So, for example, in (c) activities would be shared with husband and wife spending as much time as possible together. In the hotel study, predictably, there was a variety of working styles. In some, tasks were segregated and a husband would enter his wife's kitchen at his peril. In others, every task was shared. In the early days decisions on running the hotel are often made on the basis of personal preference. Deals are struck: "I agreed to come in if he would do the cooking"; the previous domestic style continued: "cleaning isn't a man's job, is it?" It became clear early on in the study that the term "normal working" cannot be applied. Consultants and trainers cannot take for granted that, for example, a joint organisation is natural and normal for the small hotel. Each family has its own idiosyncracies and these have to be taken into account by anyone involved in entrepreneurial development in this field.

Writers on the family discuss support systems at length. Views on aid patterns vary according to Bell(10) and Rosser and Harris(11).

The family in the hotel is no different from many others, enjoying some form of 'surreptitious help' from the extended family. More overtly, domestic help is provided from the maternal links, whilst financial support comes in a variety of forms. In some cases this involves pooling the property interests of two or more families across the generations.

This to some extent accords with Bott's view that: "perhaps women arrange visits and certain minor types of mutual aid, but when large sums of money are involved the men take over"(5).

Initiates tend to comprise solo, husband and wife, and partnership organisations. This last is particularly suitable for start-up, "collectively the four of us have the necessary skills. Each pair operates alternate shifts".

The transition from normal domestic life to living and working in a hotel is stressful for some. Medlik(3) suggests that "many units have developed from the private household and have retained many of its characteristics". Delegation is not a feature of the small firm in any industry as Perrigo reminds us:

"Delegation, or lack of it, is usually by far the most difficult for owner-managers ... (who) will have his own personal objectives as owner"(12). Given the blurred lines between family and business in a smaller hotel it is little wonder that some wives are reluctant to delegate activities to which they have been conditioned over time to regard as 'theirs'. "My wife was reluctant to give up the domestic duties and felt aggrieved that others in the family, with very little training and encouragement, could do the jobs which she had regarded as her province". After all, it's home as well as a business, and in the early days it is difficult not to think of guests as intruders!

This was a point which has recurred again in a variety of forms: "I don't like the idea of people walking around my home, you give them a key, and they can go anywhere". This could be a particular problem when it impinged on child-rearing. When mothers are busy bringing up their offspring in the home the environment has to be right. Here a more restrictive and private view of family would prevail: "I can't stand dirty, inefficient, idle or unintelligent staff working in such close proximity. They can pollute the atmosphere in which my family is growing up, and therefore have to be rooted out like weeds".

There are other shocks in store for the Initiate. "living on credit can be worrying" ... "our neighbours seem to live on a permanent loan" ... "the sheer drudgery is a lot more than we expected" ... "On paper we are worse off than we were before".

There is, however, generally an air of optimism in the Initiate's hotel ... things can only get better! A glimmer of hope of better times ahead exists for many ... it's an exciting time, the world is their oyster ... it is the spring, and the cold blasts of the winter of disillusionment are a long way off.

Hoteliers are, initially, unselective in catering for all comers. "We will take anything, children, dogs, etc" but after one or two seasons, the family is beginning to discriminate. "We'll not have an all-male party again" ... the mind boggles at that! "We'll not take children under 5" etc. It is the period for discovery. "We want to attract families ... our own can run around more freely in that atmosphere". A partnership "becoming closer-knit ... It's like a marriage between four of us". For another interviewee the split had already become inevitable ... no way will two families make a living".

As the Initiate matures so different strategies begin to emerge. Some are feeling the pressure already to move on to bigger and better things. Our Initiate has also learned during his first three seasons about the environment and the technology of the hotel or guest house in which he is operating. He learns that some things can be changed, others remain immutable ... the hotel has built-in attractions and disadvantages both for the client and the owner.

THE SMALL HOTEL

The small hotel, for the purposes of this study, comprises 11-15 letting rooms. It can provide the initiate with a chance 'to serve an apprenticeship' but, surprisingly, all types of organisations were found in control of such establishments, eg. solo, husband and wife, and partnerships. Additional staffing support ranged from a few schoolchildren on a part-time seasonal basis, to full-time staff which, in one case, totalled 14!

Hotels also have different selling biases:

(i) Accommodation (ii) Food (iii) Bar (iv) Country House

Some are "essentially a restaurant with rooms". With others ... "the bar is important here - we are the village local too". Still others see it as their role to "make up a series of house parties". Size is, therefore, not necessarily any indication of the level of services available.

Two themes, however, emerge at this size level, either (a) the desire to move on to something bigger ... "There is a limit as to how far this can go", or (b) an inclination to stay put ... "We're not chasing money. You couldn't ask for a nicer home, nice area, good relationships. A lot of hoteliers are on the make, we are not".

But 'on the make' or not, the small hotel has an important contribution to make to society: "A silly little place like this supports you, supports a lot of employees, gives people a decent holiday, and you get a whole lot of satisfaction out of it".

There are four very powerful forces pulling the family in different directions, and at this level, they can be difficult to separate. The following diagram illustrates these.

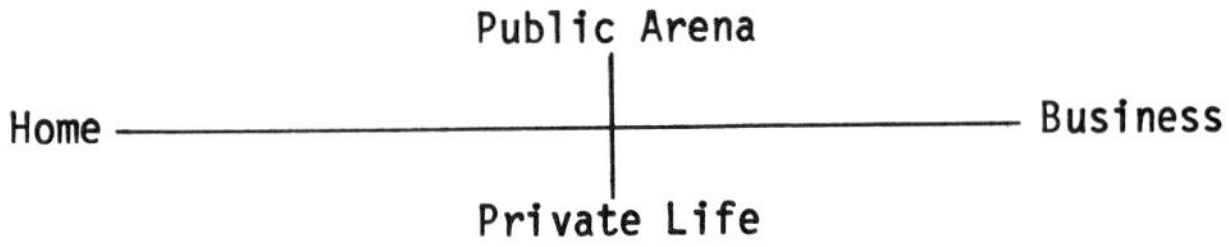

At times, the family lives in a kind of goldfish tank, from which there is no escape. During the season it can become theatrical and, for some, there are the usual first-night nerves. "I do flap internally ... may not sleep for three nights before we open ... but once it's open, it's

OK". Feelings have to be repressed in public. "You must be obliging ... give them the red carpet ... create a family atmosphere". ... "It's like show business ... you have a kitchen face and a dining-room face". The show has to go on: "you can't die in the season" ... "had a mastectomy and still survived without too much help".

It is very difficult in the small hotel with minimal staff support to distinguish the boundaries between running a domestic household and a business. "If you are a professional, you can run a hotel at one level and live at another, but as amateurs we can't do that. It's our home ... we live here".

One can sense a reluctance to get any bigger from some respondents who have mastered the technology of their own little business, have everything under control and are in no way vulnerable to the whims and moods of the unpredictable 'outsider'. It's the family name, pride and prestige which is at stake. Why trust it to anyone? "I never liked doing housework ... hated it ... the hotel idea would enable me to employ staff to do it ... I don't want that any more ... don't want to order people about and be Lady Muck ... don't want to organise other people ... this is in part due to laziness". It takes time to explain to others how to do things and to learn to accept that their standards are not yours, but that they are doing their best. Why promote oneself? "Here the staff are friends, the hotel is home ... if we were larger I wouldn't see the guests ... and I am not qualified to cook in the way a larger place would want".

Nevertheless, the small hotel develops skills in the owners and staff. There is often, particularly in the accommodation-biased hotel, little demarcation in the task structure - "We all muck in here".

In keeping with all types of working involving contact with the public, social skills are needed in both the family and in the staff. Some hoteliers who had children sent to local colleges questioned whether these skills could be imparted wholly in the college environment, and that much must relate to the basic motivation of the individual. One girl can make all the difference. The gloomiest building can be lit up by cheerful, friendly service, and occasionally a hotelier will find a 'little gem'.

> "She's one of those kind who can get up in a morning, be singing her head off, conscientious, bright and clean as a button, fresh as a daisy ... we decided to keep her all the year, instead of having two seasonal staff".

Families banish other less desirables. "Girls become pregnant, etc. They pollute the place. You give them a key - who will they bring in? What will they pinch?" The family selection process goes on filtering away the less desirable, attracting the paragons, creating the perfect environment (in the opinion of the owners).

One common stereotype of the hotel proprietor is that of the owner of a fast car, collecting antiques, touring the world periodically, having a fund of funny stories, mine genial host in the bar!

On balance the perceived reality is very different. These are some views expressed during the survey:

"Managed a holiday twice in eight seasons" ...
"Never had a wage out of it" ...
"It would have been a lot easier with a cleaner, but couldn't afford it"
"We don't get a day off" ...
"Frequently reach the point of exhaustion" ...
"Wife feels imprisoned here" ...
"For the sake of the guests we live in a fair degree of squalor" ...
"Seven-day week from 7.00 a.m. until midnight ... can't go on for ever"

To be fair the contrary view was expressed, too. Few approached the stereotypical image, but many were quietly satisfied ... "We have lots of hobbies and interests. We only work for 18 weeks. I'm educated for life, we've got inexpensive hobbies, walking, sketching, photography, tinkering on the piano, squash, badminton, this place keeps our head above water".

These views remind one of the couplet:

"Two men looked out through prison bars
One saw mud, the other stars".

MOBILITY AND IMMOBILITY

For the purpose of this section of the study, mobility has been defined as the ownership of more than one hotel consecutively since the date of initial acquisition up to the date of the study. Immobility is defined as remaining in the initial hotel. The sample comprised the following:-

M = Mobiles I = Immobiles

	Initiates		Developers		Established		Total	
FLYDE	(M)	(I)	(M)	(I)	(M)	(I)	(M)	(I)
Small	2	13	5	4	2	5	9	22
Medium	2	8	8	6	1	6	11	20
Large	1	1	2	2	5	4	8	7
Total	5	22	15	12	8	15	28	49
LAKELAND								
Small	0	4	0	15	2	11	2	30
Medium	0	5	1	6	3	12	4	23
Large	0	3	2	1	2	4	4	8
	0	12	3	22	7	27	10	61

This is in no way intended to be a statistical analysis. In the first instance, it is very difficult to ascertain the aggregate number of hotels in the various environments. Nevertheless, the above figures indicate that of the 148 hoteliers visited at random, there was predictably a greater degree of mobility amongst those who had had more experience. Similarly, owners of larger hotels tended to have run smaller establishments. The above table also confirms the intuitive feeling that there was much more movement of hoteliers in the resorts. Estate agents alert to this are known to call upon hoteliers to enquire if a move is contemplated. Some move in the first three seasons. They include families who have made an error ... "quickly realised a nine-bedder wouldn't keep us". Others are essentially involved in property deals spiraling as quickly as possible into the largest loans available.

The next major change seems to occur after 3 to 4 seasons if and when owners realise they can make a go of it. Repayment of loans after 5 - 7 seasons introduces a new taxation situation and there are incentives to burden the business with additional expenses to offset against tax.

One could hypothesise that age and attitude to change are in some way related. The following age distribution of Mobiles and Immobiles shows some interesting differences.

Age of starting	Immobiles		Mobiles		Total	
	No	%	No	%	No	%
16-20	6	6.5	-	-	6	3.7
21-25	23	24.7	-	-	23	14.1
26-30	12	12.9	20	28.2	32	19.5
31-35	7	7.5	8	11.3	15	9.1
36-40	13	14.0	20	28.2	33	20.1
41-45	19	20.4	16	22.5	35	21.3
46-50	11	11.8	4	5.6	15	9.1
51-55	2	2.2	3	4.2	5	3.1
	93	100.0	71	100.0	164	100.0

Immobiles tend to be brought into the business at an earlier age. The age range of 21-25 is particularly significant, for most of this group can have had very little experience in the industrial or commercial sector, being frequently the offspring of founder-relatives who have been brought into the family business before embarking upon another career. Mobiles manifest many of the characteristics described by Collins and Moore. Wives, particularly, tend to have had a series of occupations which have contributed pin money to the family as children have been added (e.g. as usherettes, machinists, barmaids or shop assistants). Many activities, however, involving dealing with the public have helped to build up the social skills which are to become valuable later.

The discontinuity of employment also characterised the male mobiles. We find, for example, a husband who has "tried his hand at many things - poultry farming, concreting garages, wagon driving, running a pub, etc." After carrying out the renovations, extensions, etc., i.e. once the physical challenge has been overcome, some husbands become disinterested in the running of the hotel, regarding this as essentially "women's work".

The kind of determination to get on is typified by one husband and wife team interviewed.

"In 12 years I have moved house 8 - 9 times ... each time improving the property. I had the drive, he was good with his hands." This will to succeed comes not from any intellectual assurance. One lady .... "had a thing about not being able to spell." Another respondent lost his first job because of his inability to read. Mobiles often referred to their upbringing using phrases such as "from a poorish background" .... "our family never had a lot to do out of" .... "we were a large family, many mouths to feed" .... "no car" .... "council house" .... "tenement in the poorer part of the city".

Many seemed to have lost a parent, for one reason or another, in early childhood. These family disasters had left the family "hard up". Nearly all had left school at 14 - 15, having "failed 11+" .... "gone to the usual council school" .... "secondary modern" .... "not very academic, more practical" .... "unable to read".

Ambitions on leaving school were .... "to become a nurse" .... "a hairdresser" but many were deflected by parents into "dead end jobs" such as the 'rag trade', semi-skilled work, etc. After these frustrations, ideas were to "rise above it all" .... "always wanted nice things" .... "had an aim - always wanted to get to the top, wanted to get what I wanted, clothes conscious, liked nice things, won't live in squalor." Perhaps you have to experience certain things to aspire to get out of "the drudgery of living and working in Rochdale". In such circumstances even Blackpool can represent an escape.

This drive to get on has already been identified in many other entrepreneurial studies, but the exact objectives may not be shared thoughout the family.

"My husband was starry-eyed about this business, coming from an industrial background, but I liked being my own boss". In this tiny, two-person business, there were different expectations, dreams, hopes and ambitions. There was a conflict of styles; the 'domestic' favoured by the wife, the 'managerial' by the husband, which temporarily caused some alienation in the relationship. Here the husband, wanting to alleviate "some of the drudgery" for his wife by acquiring a bigger hotel with staff, found that his wife "felt threatened" because what had been "her kitchen" was now taken over by professionals. The wife was to leave the newly-acquired business in favour of a job behind the counter of a local shop.

There seems to be a crucial stage in the development of this kind of family business, when the business changes from being essentially domestically oriented, to an economic enterprise requiring a different attitude on the part of family participants. Parsons, according to Harris(4) "assumes that extended kin are differentiated from one another in occupational terms and that people in industry act universalistically and promote and recruit on an achievement basis sufficiently often to make that differentiation a reality."

In the above example, the kitchen of that hotel has changed. It is no longer the particularistic one of the wife, but belongs to experts who are carrying out tasks because they are technically the most able (by objective professional criteria). The business has changed from a hotel employing family mainly, to the family employing specialists.

It is postulated, therefore, that there is a kind of two-stage entrepreneurial development in the family hotel business:

Stage I Domestic Style

Stage II Management Style

Similarly, it is interesting that the male from a typical industrial/commercial background brings a universalistic approach to the business, whilst in this instance the female adopts a particularistic stance. It would seem that if growth and development is to take place, this conflict has to be resolved in favour of the universalistic approach.

This could also be the work of Handy's(2) manipulative male, who can pressurize a spouse who lacks expertise into the more conventional domestic mode. One way to resolve this is to buy her a house separate from the business to occupy her as had been the case in a number of the businesses studied. Then the normal pattern of one breadwinner to a nuclear family returns, with the hotel managed by the male.

The family influence is very strong in the Immobiles. Many are 'inheritors', with the business having been in the family for years. Some have been born into the hotel, and are expected to take it over in due course.

> "It's a family tradition - the family have been in hotels for 300 years."
> "Wife's grandmother bought this in 1904"
> "Mother was born in this business in 1890".

Another major group of Immobiles comprises those who, or whose parents or relations, have already got an achievement record in business behind them.

> "Set up a confectionery business with father"
> "Dress designer, had my own business"
> "Parents had a newsagency in Keswick"
> "Father had a shop, milk round, and smallholding".

This group tended to go to private schools, grammar schools, universities, professions and serve apprenticeships. They did not have the 'drifting pattern" of the Mobiles.

Harris(4) suggests:

> "It many seem surprising that the family should, on account of its socialising function, be considered important. Surely the family is simply an agent which transmits whatever ideas go to make up the culture of society? On the contrary, it seems possible that the family firm, particularly the system of inheritance, can vitally affect those ideas .... where a child knows from birth that all he has to do is to sit back and wait to inherit, his whole activity and that of his parents is going to be directed towards fitting him for his role as inheritor, whatever that may involve."

The owners of hotels eventually have important property interests and their offsprings in consequence, are thereby affected.

> "Economic ties operate more forcibly between relatives than between friends, and neighbours .... the connectedness of the kinship network is enhanced if relatives hold property rights in common enterprises or if they expect to inherit property from one another."(4)

Several examples of parental authority backed by property interests were uncovered which substantiated this view.

> "I came into the business as a girl, nursed my grandfather until he was 95 .... wielding a big stick all the time".
> "Mum influenced me and persuaded me to come into the business. I did what I was told "

Immobility in such circumstances may make good economic (and family) sense. There are examples of dynastic family businesses operating very successfully. Conversely, death has intervened to rob a father of a son and by so doing eroded his resolve to push the business further. The inability of a son to work with his father has led to the sale of a successful business because the original investment plans assumed a time-scale which would include at least two generations whereas, "now there is no point."

There was, as seen above, a greater degree of mobility in the Fylde resorts as compared to Lakeland. This appears related to the connection between Immobiles and inheritance or family tradition involving property interests in the more stable rural environment. Harris(4) suggested that .... "the greater is the extent to which the inhabitants are limited by ties of kinship and the same class and ethnic group membership the more solidary (sic) the locality will be and more distinctive it will be vis à vis other localities." In a resort such as Blackpool there are a large number of similar units in intense competition with each other.

One respondent observed:

> "(I) miss the community life, it's not like living in a village. You don't get to know your neighbours well. We have no friends here; it's a cultural desert, especially in winter. The social cost is high."

Many reported this feeling of isolation partly because of the aggresive nature of the business and a feeling of intense competition which precluded genuine friendship. Under these circumstances, the solidarity of the family and household group (which can include regular staff), becomes stronger. Harris(4) suggests that "the more mobile they are, the less possible will it be for claims to prestige and social position to be made on particularistic grounds, since the particular people, relationships to whom provide the basis of claims to status, will not be known to the other inhabitants, and class categorisation will, therefore, be made on the basis of placement in universalistic categories on the grounds of achievement."

In a place such as a seaside resort, finite categories for such achievement have been evolved by the hotel population. The size of the property and its precise location in the town determine its turnover potential. There are few secrets. Everyone has an accurate picture of a hotel's 'worth' ... it has a price. "Oh! This is a second-time buyer hotel."

obility is inevitable for the spiralist and there are only two ways up given the nature of the seaside towns:

(a) increase in size

(b) get to the Front ... "when you've cracked it"

The aristocrats of the hotel society are thus to be found 'on the Prom'. Below (and within) this group there is a clear social order. Thus one can understand the precision of a Mobile when asked about the next move:

> "It's got to be one more move to an 18/20 bedder ... would like a place with a dance floor."

This environment contrasts with the Lakes. Their size, location and other physical factors are not the only determinants of worth. Placement in Lakeland hotel society is much more elaborate. Many have their own particularistic and highly discriminating band of followers. Each hotel has a special appeal. Some attract theatricals, Peers and others who prize privacy in order to temporarily escape their public.

In turn, such hotels as these have a fringe of followers who vicariously enjoy some of the status and prestige of this group by association: "We met ... whilst on holiday at ..."

The Lakeland environment produces hotels with high reputations for cuisine. It can take a lifetime to build up an international reputation, but there are places which have made it and these help in the formation of the aims and goals of newcomers: "We want to be like ..." In contrast to Blackpool there is no need to move from hotel to hotel in Lakeland to become socially mobile ... you can go so far on one site that ... "my family can't afford to stay here".

CONCLUSIONS

This study has highlighted the complexities of the mechanisms affecting the development of a very important aspect of our tourist industry. A feature of this is the rich variety of accommodation units throughout the UK creating opportunities for the enlightened amateur and the highly qualified professional.

The row upon row of seemingly uneconomic premises offering residential accommodation for tourists, particularly in our holiday resorts, can only be explained by some reference to the underpinning anthropological and sociological factors.

Environmental factors cannot be ignored in establishing horizons for opportunities, building a framework of aims, goals and expectations of both guests and owners. The hotel provides an ideal economic vehicle for the nuclear family which has a built-in organisational structure, with readily marketable skills. It also provides the outlet for the aspirations of key members, who are constrained by domestic responsibilities from pursuing alternative careers in society.

The hobbyist, careerist and spiralist can use the small hotel to fulfil their varying ambitions. In consequence, this tourist facility can create particular environments designed to meet the needs of a wide variety of tastes. Hotel families, staff and clients move together or in different directions in a social process, similar to that of an extended family.

The resolution of the struggle between domestic and business priorities determines the kind of developmental path which will be taken by the family and its business. This industry highlights the feature that the pursuance of particularistic goals can gain universalistic economic acclaim.

The study has particular relevance to those concerned with entrepreneurial formation and development. In this period of our history, we must not miss the opportunity to focus our attention upon the mechanisms which are significant in this. The individual entrepreneur can perhaps only be fully understood within the context of his family system, a factor which is all too often overlooked.

REFERENCES

1. Hotel and Catering EDC, Hotel Prospects to 1985, 1975.
2. Handy, C, 'Days of the Stay-at-Home Husbands', The Guardian, 11 August 1980.
3. Medlik, S, Profile of the Hotel and Catering Industry, Heinemann, 1972 (revised 1978).
4. Harris, C, The Family, Allen & Unwin, 1972.
5. Bott, E, Family and Social Network, Tavistock, 1972.
6. Ouest, Miles, How to Buy Your Own Hotel, Brodie, Marshall & Co.
7. Gove, W R, 'The Relationship between Sex Roles, Marital Status and Mental Illness' from Family Roles and Interaction, ed Heiss, J, Rand cNally, Chicago, 1976.
8. Dennis, N, Henriques, F and Slaughter, C, Coal is our Life, Eyre & Spottiswood, 1956.
9. Walton, J K, The Blackpool Landlady, Manchester University Press, 1978.
10. Bell, C, Middle Class Families, Routledge & Keegan Paul, London, 1969.
11. Rosser, C and Harris, C, The Family and Social Change, Routledge & Keegan Paul, London, 1965.
12. Perrigo, E B, 'Succession and Delegation in the Small Firm', Personnel Management, May 1975.
13. Collins, D and Moore, D G, The Organisation Makers, Appleton-Century-Crofts, New York, 1970.